Ecological Aspects of War: Religious and Theological Perspectives

A Forum for Theology in the World
Volume 3, Issue 2, 2016

A Forum for Theology in the World is an academic refereed journal aimed at engaging with issues in the contemporary world, a world which is pluralist and eucumenical in nature. The journal reflects this pluralism and ecumenism. Each edition is theme specific and has its own editor responsible for the production. The journal aims to elicit and encourage dialogue on topics and issues in contemporary society and within a variety of religious traditions. The Editor in Chief welcomes submissions of manuscripts, collections of articles, for review from individuals or institutions, which may be from seminars or conferences or written specifically for the journal. An internal peer review is expected before submitting the manuscript. It is the expectation of the publisher that, once a manuscript has been accepted for publication, it will be submitted according to the house style to be found at the back of this volume. All submissions to the Editor in Chief are to be sent to: hdregan@atf.org.au.

Each edition is available as a journal subscription, or as a book in print, pdf or epub, through the ATF Press web site — www.atfpress.com. Journal subscriptions are also available through EBSCO and other library suppliers.

Editor in Chief
Hilary Regan, ATF Press

A Forum for Theology in the World is published by ATF Theology and imprint of
ATF (Australia) Ltd (ABN 90 116 359 963) and
is published twice or three times a year.
ISSN 1329-6264

ATF Press
PO Box 504
Hindmarsh SA 5007
Australia
www.atfpress.com

Subscription Rates 2016

Print	On-Line	Print and On-line
Aust $65 Individuals	Aus $55 individuals	Aus $75 individuals
Aus $90 Institutions	Aus $80 individuals	Aus $100 instiutions

Ecological Aspects of War: Religious and Theological Perspectives

ATF Theology
Adelaide
2016

Contents

Ecological Aspects of War: Religious and Theological Perspectives from Australia
Introduction

Anne Elvey, Deborah Guess and Keith Dyer

Australian cities and suburbs present a veneer of peace as we appear to have no war on our shores and much-reported terrorist incidents remain infrequent here in practice. Nonetheless, as ANZAC day commemorations attest, war remains part of the Australian cultural imagination. Australia has officially engaged in wars for most of the years since the end of World War II in 1945—including Korea 1950–1953, Vietnam 1962–1975, Iraq 1990–91, Afghanistan 2001–present, Iraq 2003–2009, and Iraq [Operation Okra] 2014–present—and has been a partner to the U.S. in the Cold War with the USSR (1945–1991).[1]

Security anxiety has been one characteristic of an Australian cultural imaginary over this period. This anxiety has both planetary and national referents. At a planetary level, nuclear arms proliferation has exemplified a threat to the whole Earth community, prompting multiple forms of resistance including the Palm Sunday Peace rallies of the 1980s. The danger of nuclear arms, while not diminished in the post-Cold War period, has receded in the popular imagination, replaced (despite the phenomenon of climate change denial) by the reality of anthropogenic (human-induced) climate change.

Nationally, security anxiety has focused around the trope of 'border protection' and the Palm Sunday Peace rallies have become Ral-

---

1. 'Conflicts', Australian War Memorial, <https://www.awm.gov.au/conflicts/> Accessed 26 November 2016.; 'Okra home', Australian Government Department of Defence Global Operations, <http://defence.gov.au/Operations/Okra/default.asp> Accessed 26 November 2016. The opening paragraphs of this introduction draw on material in our article: Anne Elvey, Keith Dyer and Deborah Guess, 'Ecological Aspects of War: Imagining Creaturely Mission', *Australian Journal of Mission Studies* (December 2016).

lies for Refugees, where participants protest Australia's treatment of asylum seekers, especially the cruel practices of offshore detention.[2] War and state sanctioned oppression have been critical dynamics in the serious global refugee situation, which increasingly has environmental factors, including in the Western Pacific, Australia's oceanic neighbour.[3]

At the same time, in Australia ongoing colonialist policies towards Indigenous people and Country, and the pressure of mining—even where it is 'welcomed' for its economic 'benefits'—effect a violence that is arguably akin to 'war'. For novelist Tim Winton, white settler Australia has a 'siege mentality' with respect to Indigenous people and their lands.[4]

On 28 September 2015, at a conference entitled 'Ecological Aspects of War' from which the essays in this issue arose, former president of the Medical Association for the Prevention of War, Dr Jenny Grounds, spoke of 'Planet Earth as a Victim of War'. She said:

> The direct effects of war on humans are so great that the environmental effects might seem insignificant in comparison. But war also contributes greatly to environmental degradation including worsening climate change.[5]

The link between contemporary wars and climate change is one that Mick Pope takes up in his essay '"Oil and Blood on the Bayonet": Empire, Oil, War and Ecology'. Deborah Guess points out, however,

---

2. See, for example, 'Palm Sunday 2016: Walk for Justice for Refugees. March 20, 2016', Refugee Advocacy Network: A Coalition of Victorian Groups Campaigning for Rights for Refugees in Australia, <http://rac-vic.org/2016/01/23/2pm-march-20-walk-for-justice-for-refugees/> Accessed 26 November 2016

3. See, for example, Cathy Alexander, 'Climate Refugees: In the Too-Hard Basket?' Melbourne Sustainable Society Institute, University of Melbourne, <http://sustainable.unimelb.edu.au/climate-refugees> Accessed 26 November 2016; Norman Myers, 'Environmental Refugees: A Growing Phenomenon of the 21st Century', in *Philosophical Transactions of the Royal Society B: Biological Sciences*, 357 (2002): 609–13, <http://www.ncbi.nlm.nih.gov/pmc/articles/PMC1692964/pdf/12028796.pdf> Accessed 26 November 2016.

4. Tim Winton, *Island Home: A Landscape Memoir* (Docklands, VIC: Hamish Hamilton, 2015), 91–93, 95

5. Jenny Grounds, 'Planet Earth as a Victim of War', keynote address to Ecological Aspects of War: Religious Perspectives from Australia conference, 28 September 2015, Trinity College Theological School, Parkville, Victoria.

in her 'Oil beyond War and Peace: Rethinking the Meaning of Matter', that Earth might also be seen as a victim of so-called 'peace'. As Jurgen Brauer comments, 'when the guns are silent, nature does not necessarily recover because by all appearances peace (economic development) is a continuation of war on nature'.[6] For John McDowell, in his 'Political Imaginings to Cultivate Eco-Lively Reflections on Violence', the idea of a 'war' on nature may be less useful than analyses of human violence against more-than-human (including human) others, and of the deep causes of this violence.

Important to these issues of war and violence is not so much the question of the extent to which Earth is impacted by human warfare, or more generally the multiplicities of violence certain humans perpetrate against other humans, other creatures and our often shared habitats, critical though these questions are. Rather, the crucial question concerns the frame of reference we bring to thinking about ecology and war. Usually, such questions are addressed from an anthropocentric frame and with a set of barely conscious anthropocentric assumptions. While the questions of the impact of human violence on the wider Earth community are critical in themselves, what if theologians and scholars of religion were to address thinking about war and peace through the lens of the wellbeing of the entire Earth community?

In gathering the essays in this issue, we had two main aims: first to situate questions of war and peace in a wider ecological framework particularly in relation to Australia; second to bring insights from religious traditions to bear on the complex, seemingly impossible global situation which touches almost (and arguably) every people and place.

As a medical professional, Grounds spoke about the links between human health and environmental health; such links stem from and give evidence for our interconnectedness and interdependence with more-than-human beings. Moreover, the experience of peoples seeking refuge as an adaptation to climate change exemplifies the interconnectedness of social and ecological justice. Not only do humans now influence the lives and habitats of other than humans in multiple and complex ways, but the interconnectedness of social and ecologi-

---

6. Jurgen Brauer, *War and Nature: The Environmental Consequences of War in a Globalized World* (Lanham, MD: Altamira Press, 2009), 149.

cal justice highlights also the inter-influence of humans and their own habitats. Humans are embedded in more-than-human habitats, affecting and affected by the interconnected fates of more-than-human others.

Concerns about human security, then, are ill-founded if they are not embedded in wider concerns for more-than-human others and for Earth itself. 'We have a very narrow and simplistic concept of security', Grounds said. She noted that the kinds of security fears that took shape in the twenty-first century, particularly after 9/11, were a setback for action on climate change and nuclear disarmament. Nonetheless, argued Grounds, as 'intelligent beings', humans are not only 'responsible for our behaviour toward others and the environment', but also that we have the capacity to act with and for the good of the planet. 'We have developed ways to encourage and enforce good habits, and to prevent crimes and antisocial behaviour', she said. For Grounds, these ways include religious traditions and systems of law. Her activist challenge to theologians and scholars of religion was to articulate these ways in terms of a planetary good.

In different ways, the contributors to this issue take up this challenge. In his essay 'Ecology and Peace: Responding to the Ethos of Exclusion', Joseph Camilleri comments:

> What renders the present situation unacceptable are not simply the symptoms of our contemporary ailment, be it carbon emissions or casualties on the battlefield, but the underlying psychological and social structures that exclude, whether it be on the basis of identity as defined by gender, sexual orientation, class, caste, race, ethnicity, religion, culture or ideology, or on the basis of dualisms that separate mind and body, matter and spirit, the human species and other living systems.

Drawing on Pope Francis' encyclical *Laudato Si'* and other contemporary prophetic voices, Camilleri calls for a radical inclusivity in the 'new' epoch toward which we as humans are moving. He labels this 'the holoreflexive epoch', a planetary, ecocentric time which 'represents, at least embryonically, a holistic response to the logic of exclusion' in its embrace of 'the totality of relationships between the human species and the rest of the biosphere'.

Like Camilleri, McDowell is concerned with the structures—social, cultural, political—that promote and authorise violence. He begins with the idea that there are habitual pathologies associated with the 'death-drive' which give rise to systemic violence. Drawing on the 'conflictual ontologies' found in literary images from a diverse group of writers—Nietzsche, Shelley and Euripides—McDowell suggests that the underlying preoccupation with death and violence can be exposed and fractured. Cultivating theologian Grace Jantzen's 'life giving metaphor of natality' offers an alternative version of cultural politics.

Life-giving is implicit in Shelini Harris's approach to non-violence. In her essay 'Our War with Nature and Each Other from a Buddhist Perspective', Harris makes strong connections between human conflict and our attitudes to nature. Both types of conflict, Harris argues, derive from our inability to recognise the interrelatedness of all life. Particularly in Western culture this has led to an ethic of power and control over nature. Drawing on Sharon Welch and Vandana Shiva, Harris argues from a Buddhist perspective that a greater understanding and appreciation of the relationship between humans and other forms of life may enable us to relinquish the urge to control and so invite non-violent ways of living, both with each other and with the Earth.

Deborah Guess builds on the new materialism to suggest a Christological basis for such understanding and appreciation of the relationships between humans and other beings, not simply other forms of life. She calls into question a 'life/matter' dualism, by affirming with thinkers such as Jane Bennett the agency of matter. Moving beyond the generally secular approach of new materialist studies, Guess argues that the concept of 'deep incarnation' offers a basis for rethinking not only divine relationship with more-than-humans but more particularly the way matter has agency in matters of war and peace. Taking the example of 'the spillage and firing of oil in the Gulf War of 1991', Guess asks:

> how might our actions change if we see the spillage, even the extraction, of oil, whether as the consequence of the workings of our peace-time economy or as an act of war, as similarly involving something which is not only a resource/fuel for human consumption but also, like garbage, is 'lively and potentially dangerous'?

Thinking about matter as active and ourselves as coagents with other matter, in an incarnational context where Christ is deeply embedded in the material world, unsettles the problematic dualisms that support human domination of the rest of creation. Moreover, this unsettling suggests a more complex way of thinking about our impact as part of the natural world that decentres human agency.

Such decentring of human agency does not take away human responsibility, but does suggest a kenotic approach to human response to violence. In her essay, 'Bonhoeffer and "the right to self assertion": Understanding Theologically the Mastery of Nature and War', Dianne Rayson takes up Dietrich Bonhoeffer's theme of self-assertion, understood as the assertion of rights over against the rights of others. Although Bonhoeffer discussed the theme in relation to the violence of war, Rayson argues that Bonhoeffer's ideas on assertion can also be extended to a discussion of violence in relation to ecology. This is possible because war and ecology are 'connected at a conceptual level where theological interrogation of mastery, power and violence can occur'. Bonhoeffer's insight that there is a contrast between the Eastern way (surrender) and the Western way (mastery) can lead, Rayson argues, to a Christian kenotic way of responding to, and preventing, both the violence of war and violence against Earth.

In what ways do religious traditions negotiate these questions of response to and prevention of violence in practice? Lawyer, Asmi Wood takes up this question in relation to Islamic Law with reference to International Humanitarian Law (IHL) in his essay 'Some Limits to the Use of Armed Force under the *Sharia*'. In a contemporary context where radical militant groups such as IS claim allegiance to Islam, Wood explores in careful detail the provisions and prohibitions on engagements with the 'enemy', non-combatants, and treatment of prisoners of war in armed conflict and examines the lawfulness of certain practices claimed by such groups as being permissible under Islamic law. At the same time, Wood suggests that aspects of Islamic law could helpfully inform IHL. He proposes a form of words for contemporary *sharia* law in relation to war, including a focus on other creatures. Under Islamic law, other animals should not be killed except for food. The Islamic prohibition of fire as a means of war has implications for the use of many modern forms of weaponry, and Wood argues that based on this prohibition: 'Muslims should take the opportunity to use *sharia* norms to join in and promote weapons ban treaties, particularly weapons that cause slow painful deaths to animals and humans.'

Mick Pope's essay, mentioned above, is the final essay in this issue and considers a biblical Christian response to the violence of empires. Pope, with a background in mathematics, science and meteorology, carefully and passionately describes intersections between oil, climate change, wars in the Middle East in recent centuries, and U.S. imperialism. He then draws on contemporary biblical scholarship, to consider responses to empire, in early Christian writings of the first century CE, with a particular focus on Pauline letters. He argues that: 'Paul's declaration of the gospel in Rom 1:1–5 is anti-empire … presenting Jesus as the world's true Lord in contradistinction to Caesar.' For Pope, the 'Lordship of Christ' has practical implications for twenty-first century Christians who are called to ecological and social justice in this pressing context of the geopolitical impacts of oil. It is 'a matter of Christian duty to repay the historical debts incurred by fossil fuel extraction and use.' The 'Pax Christi' becomes a kind of yardstick which 'is nothing like the Pax Romana or Pax Americana.' The peace of Christ is counter-imperial and implies such practices as 'a sharing of energy technologies' to 'help replace the violent acquisition of energy resources that now takes place.'

As each of the contributors to this volume attests, there is no simple description of the impacts and causes of the violence of war and the violence against the planet, or their intersection. The complexity of the situation invites humility. The entanglement of humans with other creatures, with their own habitats and with the habitats of others far from them, implies a decentring of humankind, especially of Western notions of human supremacy, and a conversion from anthropocentrism in activism, theology and religious discourse. Religious traditions, while sometimes seen as part of the problem, offer ways of countering the ideologies and imaginaries of human mastery, through kenotic, life-affirming and inclusive orientations toward peace. There is a long way to go, but the task for scholars is to engage their own traditions alongside those of others in multidisciplinary, inter-faith conversation. Scholarship in this area will necessarily be a form of activism and will call forth cooperation with activists for justice, peace and ecological wholeness in what Camilleri calls 'the holoreflexive epoch' where we affirm and embrace the planetary relationality of which we are part.

Although not often seen in this way, one aspect of the planetary relationality of which we are part is our scholarly collegiality. We are grateful not only to the contributors for sharing their scholarship in this volume, especially to Associate Professor Asmi Wood for sharing his expertise in Islamic and International law at our invitation. We very much appreciate the work of our anonymous referees who peer reviewed the other six essays in this volume. Finally, the Ecological Aspects of War conference in 2015 and early work on this project was enabled by a small research grant from the University of Divinity, and the support in kind of Trinity College Theological School, Whitley College and the Yarra Institute for Religion and Social Policy. We offer our thanks.

Ecology and Peace: Responding to the Ethos of Exclusion

Joseph A Camilleri

In the aftermath of the Second World War it seemed as if the most troubling contradictions identified by the critics of industrialism were on the way to resolution. Within the space of fifteen years much of the Western world was enjoying a steady increase in consumption, full or close to full employment, vastly improved public services, including health, education and transportation, and a firmly established social safety net. This improvement in the human condition suffered, however, from two limitations: it bypassed a large fraction of humanity, notably in the Third World; and even in the industrialised world the welfare state would soon have to contend with the pressures of stagflation, rising unemployment and periodic financial crises.

During this same period, a new upheaval would emerge, one even more far-reaching, whose effects were universal and possibly irreversible. The environmental crisis, as it came to be known, gave rise to the 'limits to growth' thesis popularised by the Club of Rome,[1] which raised serious doubts as to whether the availability of natural resources (in terms of cost and accessibility) would keep pace with projected rates of economic growth. Over time the perceived scarcity of oil and water became especially troubling. The more serious limitation, however, had to do less with resource scarcity than with the disruption of the planet's delicate ecosystems established over evolutionary time scales. Environmental concerns now encompassed the totality of the environment: from ozone depletion to deforestation,

---

1. *The Limits to Growth*, a report for the Club of Rome's Project on the Predicament of mankind by Donnella H Meadows, Dennis L Meadows, Jorgen Randers, William W Behrens (London: Earth Island, 1972).

desertification, land degradation, accumulation of toxic and hazardous wastes, pollution of air, water and soil, acid rain, and loss of biodiversity. In time mounting scientific evidence would point to the reality of climate change and the devastating impact this would have on ecology, economy, society and the international order.

Even from this cursory statement of the scale and intensity of the environmental crisis it should be apparent that religion faces a challenge of unprecedented dimensions. Religion, almost by definition, may be understood as a human response to the limitations of earthly reality. It seeks to overcome these limitations by providing a path to self-transformation and spiritual fulfilment, and as part of this to offer a cosmology that gives meaning and content to human existence in both its personal and social contexts. As Mary Evelyn Tucker and John Grim suggest, religions bring to the task 'cosmological stories, symbol systems, ritual practices, ethical norms, historical processes, and institutional structures'.[2] Notwithstanding the richness of religious experience, belief and wisdom, it is fair to say that nothing before or since the Axial Age has quite prepared the world's major religions to respond to the enormity of the contemporary ecological challenge.

War and ecological disruption: deadly connections

Religion's resonance and relevance owe much to its capacity to interpret the death-rebirth cycle and guide human behaviour in ways which account for yet move beyond pain, anguish and transience. But as we shall see, the ecological crisis threatens the possibility of rebirth and in the process stunts the capacity for ethical agency. The centrality of the relationship with nature to the current human predicament must not, however, be allowed to obscure the other equally troubling dimensions of that predicament. Foremost among these is the violence that humans have unleashed against each other in the course of the last hundred or more years. The destruction, actual and threatened, of human lives has been relentless and pervasive: two world wars, the Holocaust, Hiroshima and Nagasaki, and since 1945

2. Mary Evelyn Tucker and John Grim, 'Overview of World Religions and Ecology', Yale Forum on Religion and Ecology, 2009 <http://fore.yale.edu/religion/>. Accessed 26 November 2016.

the Cold War, a succession of regional and global crises, civil and inter-state wars, genocides and bloody revolutions, and now terrorism, the 'war on terror' and the threat of total nuclear devastation that shows no sign of abating.

In some respects, the mass atrocities associated with organised violence by one state against another and at least as often by the state against its own people pose an acute ethical challenge to religion. For in this case, the suffering that is inflicted is premeditated and often perpetrated in full knowledge of the consequences, whereas the impact of environmental change may be said to have been, at least initially, largely unforeseen, and the unintended consequence of behaviour and policies pursued for other ends.

Three other facets of war-making have equally ominous ethical implications. The first is the close connection between violence and social and economic injustice. Much of the bloodletting in war is directed to expanding or defending the privileged position of military establishments, political elites, arms manufacturers and other corporate interests, often at the expense of civilian populations and the poor. The second is the speed and secrecy with which decisions to wage war are made, most dramatically manifested in nuclear decision-making. Electorates and even policy elites are thereby deprived of the capacity to make ethically informed let alone democratically accountable judgments.

The third aspect of war-making, insufficiently appreciated, is its direct and far-reaching impact on the natural and human environment. All three stages of warfare (preparation for war, war-fighting and post-war) have significant ecological consequences. Modern war preparation requires massive research programs, extensive weapons testing, military exercises, training, and construction of elaborate installations and facilities. The consequences, unintended though they may be, include residual unexploded ordnance, chemical contamination, cratering, noise pollution, vegetation removal, soil erosion, economic disruption, illnesses, and accidental death. War itself is distinguished by immense and concentrated energy flows, severe disturbances, habitat destruction, wholesale killing (including but not limited to *Homo sapiens*) and disorganisation of existing social and economic systems. Post-war conditions invariably involve intense pollution, unexploded ordnance, damaged and destroyed infrastructure, degraded landscapes and ecosystem services, economic disruption, mass refugee flows, and long-term physical illnesses and prolonged mental and emotional disorders.

When it comes to nuclear weapons, the impact, is both actual and potential. The first use of the weapon over Hiroshima and Nagasaki in 1945 amply demonstrated the catastrophic scale of death and destruction it can inflict (a combined total of 230,000 fatalities by the end of 1945), the speed with which its effects can be felt, and their widespread and persistent toxicity in the environment. The International Physicians for the Prevention of Nuclear War has estimated that some 2.4 million people will eventually die as a result of the atmospheric nuclear tests conducted between 1945 and 1980, which were equal in force to 29,000 Hiroshima bombs. These tests have involved radioactive contamination of the marine and terrestrial ecosystems through the transfer of radionuclides into the geospheres and their accumulation in living cells, by way of the food chain.[3] As for a future nuclear war, even a small number of nuclear explosions over modern cities would kill tens of millions of people. In a major nuclear confrontation between the United States and Russia, a less improbable scenario than many have assumed, casualties would reach hundreds of millions in a matter of hours. Less than one per cent of the world's nuclear arsenals would be enough to disrupt the global climate and cause nuclear famine. A major nuclear exchange involving no more than 10 per cent of the Russian and U.S. arsenals could bring about a nuclear winter and destroy the essential ecosystems on which life depends.

Climate change and nuclear deterrence are different expressions of the same destructive logic. Though the impact may differ in form and timescale, they both express the same unprecedented capacity to wipe out not only the human species but countless other animal and plant species. Nor are these just parallel phenomena. They are inextricably linked—physically, socially and theologically—and so are peace and ecological sustainability.

The Dynamics of Exclusion: Theological Perspectives

From the standpoint of religious faith—specifically the Christian understanding of creation—both mass killing and degradation of the

---

3. Remus Prăvălie, 'Nuclear Weapons Tests and Environmental Consequences: A Global Perspective', *Ambio*, 43/6 (October 2014): 729–44.

planetary environment call into question the relationship between heaven, humanity and nature. The development of Christian ecotheology over the last fifty years is one attempt to make sense of this looming rupture. Writing in 1967, Lynn White ascribed to Christianity 'a huge burden of guilt' for ecological destruction.[4] Though the root causes can be loosely attributed to sin, different views emerge when it comes to specifying the nature and attributes of the sin in question. Ernst Conradie points to the general characterisations of the sin as pride, greed, sloth or the privation of the good. He goes on to list such historical currents as the industrial revolution, the advance of science and technology and the advent of modernity. More enlightening perhaps is the reference to attitudes and values encapsulated by such notions as the logic of domination, anthropocentrism, or alienation and homelessness.[5] Writing a year after White, Thomas Merton was more explicit, describing American capitalist culture as 'firmly rooted in a secularized Christian myth and mystique of struggle with nature', according to which self-worth depends on 'overcoming and dominating the natural world'.[6] Atomic waste and the destruction of forests were but two expressions of the mystique of exploitation.

Half a century later in his encyclical *Laudato Si'* Pope Francis offers us what is perhaps the most compelling theological account yet of the contemporary ecological crisis. Drawing on the symbolic and narrative language in the Genesis accounts of creation he discerns three closely interlinked relationships—'with God, with our neighbour and with the earth itself' (*LS* 66)—as fundamental to human existence and its historical reality. Using a strictly non-literalist biblical hermeneutic, he makes the theologically radical claim that human life, indeed spiritual life, is centrally defined by the human-earth relationship. In a sense, he is arguing that the relationship with God is necessarily mediated through our relationship with our human brothers and sisters on the one hand and with 'Mother Earth' on the other. The encyclical reinterprets the account in Genesis, which

---

4. Lynn White, 'The Historical Roots of Our Ecological Crisis', *Science* (10 March 1997): 1203–7.

5. Ernst Conradie, 'The Journey of Doing Christian Ecotheology: A Collective Mapping of the Terrain', *Theology*, 116/1 (2013): 7–8.

6. Thomas Merton, 'The Wild Places', *Center Magazine* 1/5 (July 1968), reprinted in *Thomas Merton, Selected Essays*, edited by Patrick F. O'Connell (New York: Orbis Books, 2013), 444.

speaks of humans having 'dominion' over the Earth, stating emphatically that 'the bible has no place for a tyrannical anthropocentrism unconcerned for other creatures'(*LS* 68).[7] The biblical texts, we are reminded,

> tell us to 'till and keep' the garden of the world (cf. Gen 2: 15). 'Tilling' refers to cultivating, ploughing or working, while 'keeping' means caring, protecting, overseeing and preserving. This implies a relationship of mutual responsibility between human beings and nature. (*LS* 67)

In contrast to the incorrect reading of Genesis, which places the accent on exploitation of nature, the encyclical points to God's omnipresence in nature:

> The universe unfolds in God, who fills it completely. Hence, there is a mystical meaning to be found in a leaf, in a mountain trail, in a dewdrop, in a poor person's face. The ideal is not only to pass from the exterior to the interior to discover the action of God in the soul, but also to discover God in all things. (*LS* 233)

The Encyclical's powerful invocation of the dignity of nature did not emerge in a vacuum. A good deal of theological reflection that preceded it pointed in the same direction. Jürgen Moltmann's contribution spanning nearly half a century has been especially notable for its acknowledgement that the concept of rule over the Earth (*dominium terrae*) has helped to legitimate the 'expansion culture' of the Modern West, 'the subjugation of nature' and 'the instrumentalization of bodiliness'. He develops the argument further, suggesting that in European culture the divine was associated with the realm of the spiritual as against the material, with 'the historical rather than the natural', and with 'the male rather than the female'. Christianity must therefore share a good deal of the responsibility for 'the ecological crisis into which the Western expansion culture is bringing the earth.'[8] Theological renewal conveys a clear message: by recovering

---

7. *Encyclical Letter Laudato Si' of The Holy Father Francis on Care for Our Common Home*, Vatican Press, 24 May 2015 (abbreviated as *LS*), pars 66–68.
8. Jürgen Moltmann, *The Ethics of Hope*, translated by Margaret Kohl (London: SCM Press, 2012), 135–6.

the ancient wisdom of the sacred texts we are better able to respond to the formidable challenge of our times.

Complementing and deepening this renewed biblical understanding of the meaning of the created universe is the powerful focus provided by liberation theology. For Francis engagement with God's creation must rest on social justice, but more than that it has to express a profound empathy with the poor, the weak and the vulnerable. This is not to be understood as a mere add-on to biocentric and ecocentric ethics. Rather it is to frame a necessarily holistic approach to the heaven-humanity-nature nexus. In line with Leonardo Boff, Francis is intent on connecting the cry of the Earth's oppressed and marginalised with the cry of the Earth itself.

As Boff puts it, 'Liberation theology and ecological discourse have something in common: they stem from two wounds that are bleeding.'[9] Both wounds—poverty and wretchedness on the one hand and the depredations of the planet on the other—are pointing to the need for liberation. In liberation theology, the poor occupy centre stage in the sense that they are at the centre of any attempt to define the concept of God, of grace, of human history, of the church's mission. In the poor we come face to face with the reality of suffering, which is both dramatic and problematic. The encounter cannot be authentic unless it is steeped in the experience of *'com-passion'* (suffering with)—which may be considered the first stage. From being a witness to the reality of suffering emerges a second stage: the need and desire to form a *judgment*, to understand the causes of suffering. Poverty is neither natural nor pre-ordained. Exploitation and impoverishment are the result of economic and social arrangements, political institutions and cultural orientations. On such understanding rests the possibility of the third stage: *transformative action*. It is the task of Christian faith together with others similarly disposed to engage in transforming the structures and relationships of injustice. Boff posits a fourth stage, *celebration*; for whatever is achieved socially, economically or politically anticipates the advent of the 'Kingdom' understood as 'divine redemption' mediated through 'historical-social liberation'.[10]

---

9. Leonardo Boff, 'Liberation Theology and Ecology: Alternative, Confrontation or Complementarity?', in *Ecology and Poverty: Cry of the Earth, Cry of the Poor*, edited by Leonardo Boff and Virgil Elizondo (Maryknoll, NY: Orbis Books, 1995), 67.
10. Boff, 'Liberation Theology and Ecology', 72–3.

The plundering of nature and the call to action to preserve it conform to the same fundamental logic. In Boff's words:

> The same logic of the ruling system, based on profit and social manipulation, that leads to the exploitation of workers also leads to the spoliation of entire nations and eventually to the depredation of nature itself.[11]

It is here that is revealed the full significance of exploitation, be it exploitation of the environment or exploitation of people, be it fossil fuel profligacy or nuclear deterrence. Such exploitation is the inevitable outcome of the logic of exclusion, which *Laudato Si'* is at pains to expose. People and nature, and importantly future generations, are routinely excluded from the decisions likely to adversely affect them. They are excluded from decision-making processes and institutions because to include them would in all likelihood produce outcomes inconsistent with stark inequalities of wealth, income and influence. The politics of exclusion rests then on a dual mechanism, simultaneously psychological and structural, of domination and indifference. The powerful and privileged are intent on dominating in order to preserve their power and privilege, while they remain indifferent to the harm that such domination inevitably leaves in its train. It is this blend of domination and indifference, and its technocratic manifestation in economy and warfare, which threatens future generations and risks producing a planet of 'debris, desolation and filth'.[12]

The refugee, fleeing war, poverty and environmental disaster, is in many ways the quintessential victim of exclusion, and its twin progenitors, domination and indifference. In his celebrated homily delivered in Lampedusa, Pope Francis identified indifference as the key to the callous treatment of refugees and asylum seekers by the rich and comfortable:

> The culture of comfort, which makes us think only of ourselves, makes us insensitive to the cries of other people, makes us live in soap bubbles which, however lovely, are insubstantial; they offer a fleeting and empty illusion which results in indifference to others; indeed, it even leads to the

---

11. Boff, 'Liberation Theology and Ecology', 73.
12. Boff, 'Liberation Theology and Ecology', 119.

> *globalization of indifference.* In this globalized world, we have
> fallen into *globalized in difference* (italics added).[13]

Simply put, the mechanism of exclusion violently disrupts social and ecological systems. It is in its essence divisive, setting humanity against nature and fragmenting humanity into competing and warring classes, castes, communities and nations.

The logic of exclusion is itself a sign of the extraordinary upheaval that characterises every facet of life in the Modern period, and which has prompted many perceptive observers to speak of a spiritual crisis. Merton calls it 'the sickness of disordered love', a 'self-love that realizes itself simultaneously to be self-hate, and instantly becomes a source of universal, indiscriminate destructiveness'.[14] For Merton, the twentieth century world crisis, while it is grounded in ideologies of hatred and illegitimate structures of power and wealth, is experienced personally as profound alienation—alienation from self, society, nature, and ultimately from God.

The Peace-Ecology Nexus

Respect for the integrity of creation is the only plausible antidote to the dynamic of exclusion. To recognise that the universe is a sign and revelation of the divine presence is to accept that the world is inhabited by the sacred, and that all that exists in it is integrally connected by that presence and shares in that sacredness. It follows that a truly ecological response is *ipso facto* a social response, where care for the environment is indistinguishable and inseparable from the respectful and harmonious interaction of polities, cultures and religions. Hearing the cries of the Earth requires that we also hear the cries of the poor, the vulnerable and the persecuted. Against the backdrop of the Vietnam War, with crop poisoning, the defoliation of forest trees, the incineration of villages and their inhabitants with napalm, Merton

---

13. 'Visit to Lampedusa: Homily Of Holy Father Francis, 8 July 2013' <http:// w2.vatican.va/content/francesco/en/homilies/2013/documents/papa-francesco_20130708_omelia-lampedusa.html>. Accessed 26 November 2016.
14. Thomas Merton, *Conjectures of a Guilty Bystander* (Garden City, NY: Doubleday, 1965), 55.

could see with remarkable clarity that 'the ecological conscience is also essentially a peace making conscience'.[15]

The peace-ecology nexus, while it rests firmly on metaphysical foundations, is equally evident in the requirements of praxis. Climate change, ozone depletion, ocean acidification, loss of biodiversity and genetic engineering are among the many pressing environmental challenges that exceed the reach and resources of any one state. Only shared environmental problem solving holds any prospect of success. The cooperative ethic needed to prevent damaging and potentially irreversible environmental impacts cannot but have a helpful spillover effect when it comes to other arenas of peace building and conflict resolution. Ken Conca, Alexander Carius and Geoffrey Dabelko refer to three types of environmental peace making: a) conflict prevention in relation to environmental issues; b) dialogue between disputing parties; and c) attempts to establish a sustainable framework conducive to peace.[16] Christos Kyrou takes the argument a step further and suggests that many environmental practices have useful peace building potential regardless of the specifics of the problem they are addressing. In this context he cites eco-museums, environmental education, peace camps, ecovillages and eco-literary and other artistic works.[17] This theme is now well elaborated in a growing body of literature premised on the close interaction of the social and ecological realms and the transnational scope of environmental and other security challenges.[18] The ecological contribution to peace building and peace making is also evidenced in the long-term horizons needed for environmental problem solving, the emphasis placed on the contribution of local and civil society organisations, and 'the

---

15. Thomas Merton, 'The Wild Places', in *Preview of the Asian Journey*, edited by Walter Capps (New York: Crossroad, 1989), 107 reprinted from *Center Magazine*, 1/5 (July 1968).

16. Ken Conca, Alexander Carius and Geoffrey B Dabelko, 'Building Peace through Environmental Cooperation', in World Watch Institute, *State of the World 2005— Redefining Global Security* (Washington, DC: Norton, 2005), 150–2.

17. Christos N Kyrou, 'Peace Ecology: An Emerging Paradigm in Peace Studies', *Journal of Peace Studies*, 12/1 (Spring–Summer 2007): 77–8.

18. Randall Amster, 'A Sustainable Peace: From Militarized Borders to Transnational Resource Collaboration', *Journal of Sustainability Education* (19 March 2012) <http://www.jsedimensions.org/wordpress/content/a-sustainable-peace-from-militarized-borders-to-transnational-resource-collaboration_2012_03/>. Accessed 26 November 2016.

creation of commonalities that transcend the polarization caused by economic relations'.[19]

The drive to ecological sustainability, including the redesign of our modes of consumption and production, urban landscapes and agricultural systems, can no doubt lower the intensity of conflict and conversely enhance our capacity for conflict resolution. Similarly, disarmament and arms control agreements, zones of peace, post-conflict reconstruction efforts and the like can no doubt help create conditions more conducive to sustainable living. But there is much more to the ecology-peace nexus than these linkages would suggest. If the despoliation of nature and the construction of war machines that typify modern industrialism have their roots in the logic of exclusion, then what connects the sustainable use of the earth's resources and the peaceful resolution of geopolitical and ideological differences is the logic of inclusion. What renders the present situation unacceptable are not simply the symptoms of our contemporary ailment, be it carbon emissions or casualties on the battlefield, but the underlying psychological and social structures that exclude, whether it be on the basis of identity as defined by gender, sexual orientation, class, caste, race, ethnicity, religion, culture or ideology, or on the basis of dualisms that separate mind and body, matter and spirit, the human species and other living systems. Peace and ecology can therefore come together only on the basis of a renewed holistic understanding of the human journey across both space and time—a journey that encompasses the whole of humanity in all its diversity and all of its connections to the creative energy of the Cosmos. Here precisely lies the link between the peace-sustaining ethos of cultural diversity and the life-sustaining force of biodiversity, the connection being integral to the eschatological dimension of the human journey.

---

19. Alexander Carius, 'Environmental Cooperation as an Instrument of Crisis Prevention and Peace building: Conditions for Success and Constraints', paper submitted to the 2006 Berlin Conference on the Human Dimensions of Global Environmental Change, 'Resources Policies: Effectiveness, Efficiency, and Equity', Berlin, 17–18 November 2006 (October 2006) <http://userpage.fu-berlin.de/ffu/akumwelt/bc2006/papers/Carius_Peacemaking.pdf>. Accessed 26 November 2016.

Theology in the Anthropocene: scope and limitations

Climate change, the result of rapidly rising carbon emissions over the last hundred years, now points to global warming of the earth's atmosphere, rising sea levels and extreme weather events of increasing frequency and intensity. In the Pacific islands, described as the 'ground zero' of climate change, a barrage of cyclones, floods, storm surges and droughts has already unleashed a human exodus, especially from small island nations such as Tuvalu and Nauru, with far worse to follow in coming years.[20] Yet climate change is but the most dramatic manifestation of the human impact on the earth's ecosystems. Large scale soil erosion, deforestation, rapid rates of species extinction, resource depletion and waste dumping are just some of the other human induced changes to the Earth's system which have prompted a number of scientists to posit the advent of the Anthropocene,[21] a new epoch in the geological time scale, the successor to the Holocene Age which began at the end of the Ice Age some 12,000 years ago and whose climate has remained stable for the last 10,000 years until the global warming now underway.[22] The scientific body responsible for naming geological epochs, the International Commission on Stratigraphy, is soon expected to pronounce on the matter.

Regardless of geological nomenclature it is clear that the human species has itself become a powerful 'force of nature' with far-reaching ramifications not just for geology and climate but also for society, economy and culture. The industrial project rested on the principle that machines could be harnessed to understand and mould nature and in so doing predict and control the human environment. The mechanisation of agriculture could so increase output as to allow the mass exodus from the countryside to the city, where a never ending

---

20. See CSIRO, Australian Bureau of Meteorology and SPREP, 'Climate in the Pacific: A Regional Summary of New Science and Management Tools', Pacific-Australia Climate Change Science and Adaptation Planning Program Summary Report (Melbourne: Commonwealth Scientific and Industrial Research Organisation, 2015).

21. The term 'Anthropocene' was first introduced by Paul Crutzen and Eugene Stoermer, 'The "Anthropocene"', *IGBP Newsletter*, 41 (May 2000): 17–18.

22. Clive Hamilton, François Gemenne and Christophe Bonneuil, 'Thinking the Anthropocene', in *The Anthropocene and the Global Environmental Crisis: Rethinking Modernity in a New Epoch*, edited by Clive Hamilton, François Gemenne and Christophe Bonneuil (London: Routledge, 2015), 3.

spiral of scientific and technological innovation would sustain ever increasing levels of production and consumption. But this seemingly boundless drive to master and exploit nature in pursuit of human ends would soon produce a blow back effect. It is as if nature would rebel and, by its very vulnerability, begin to impose limits on economic growth and on the very capacity of culture and technical skill to limit or control the adverse environmental effects that human intervention had produced.

In the face of these extraordinary developments, religion generally and theology in particular were faced with an unprecedented challenge. Leading theologians now saw the need to place God's creation and the relationship between humanity and nature at the core of theological reflection. These efforts, spread across all major Christian traditions, have paved the way for what may loosely be called ecotheology.[23] The aim is no longer to place the environmental crisis at the centre of environmental ethics or insert it as a theme in systematic or biblical theology but to develop a comprehensive field of theological inquiry centred on the ecological crisis in this historically unique moment.[24] Some are even tempted to place ecotheology explicitly within the framework of the Anthropocene.[25] Given the prospect of catastrophic and perhaps irreversible change in the Earth's ecology, these are understandable attempts to endow theology with renewed relevance.

The very scale of the environmental crisis has prompted some to revisit the place of eschatology in theological inquiry, and to shift the centre of gravity from the individual to the species and importantly to the universe at large. The personal dimension remains but is now viewed from the vantage point of the fate of the cosmos and the possibility of an imminent end to life as we have known it during the Holocene. The possibility of climate change producing an imminent

---

23. See Ernst Conradie, Sigurd Bergmann, Celia Deane-Drummond and Denis Edwards (eds), *Christian Faith and the Earth: Current Paths and Emerging Horizons in Ecotheology* (London: Bloomsbury T&T Clark, 2014).
24. Michael S Northcott and Peter M Scott (eds), *Systematic Theology and Climate Change: Ecumenical Perspectives* (London: Routledge, 2014).
25. Clive Pearson, 'Is It Too Late? Doing Theology in the Anthropocene', paper presented at public seminar, Centre for Theology and Public Issues, University of Otago, 16 December 2015 <http://www.otago.ac.nz/ctpi/otago419801.pdf>. Accessed 26 November 2016.

tipping point raises the profoundly disturbing question of how the person of faith responds to that possibility, how the future should be understood and lived in the present. If a critical threshold has already been, or soon will be, reached, where is Christian hope to be placed, and what are the implications for both personal and social ethics?

The framing of the questions suggests a timely, perhaps radical turn in our understanding of religious faith and practice, and a holistic approach to the theology of creation.[26] The reformist impulse, however, is partially blunted by a residual tendency to integrate the eschatological implications of climate change and geological thresholds into familiar theological frames of reference, whether it be Christological accounts of salvation and redemption or Trinitarian notions of divine oneness.[27] This attachment to doctrinal orthodoxy can make it difficult to diagnose the full significance of geological and climatological transitions (*chronos*) and even more difficult to articulate a compelling vision of the historical moment when eternity erupts and a new burst of creative energy transforms the world (*kairos*).

Perhaps a more serious impediment to rethinking the role of religion and widening theological horizons is the tendency in much of ecotheology to interpret the present moment in purely or largely ecological terms. Even if it is the case that we are moving towards a new geological age, the Anthropocene, it cannot be assumed that the adverse impact of economic activity on the natural environment,

---

26. Justin Cannon, 'Exploring Ecotheology: Toward a Christian Theology of Creation', *Eco Theo Review* (14 August 2014) <http://www.ecotheo.org/2014/08/exploring-ecotheology-toward-a-christian-theology-of-creation/>.

27. Even in Moltman's case, where the clear intent is to contribute to a new theological architecture and an ecological reformation of Christianity and society, there remains a strong attachment to traditional conceptions of the resurrection of Christ crucified, the struggle with Satan, and the Trinitarian conception of God. See the following works by Jürgen Moltmann: *History and the Triune God: Contributions to Trinitarian Theology*, translated by John Bowden (London: SCM, 1991; 'The Presence of God's Future: The Risen Christ', *Anglican Theological Review*, 89/4 (2007): 577–88. See also, Neils Henry Gregerson, 'Christology', in *Systematic Theology and Climate Change*, edited by Michael S Northcott and Peter M Scott (London: Routledge, 2014), 33–50; and Denis Edwards, 'Where on Earth is God: Exploring an Ecological Theology of the Trinity in the Tradition of Athanasius', in *Christian Faith and the Earth: Current Paths and Emerging Horizons in Ecotheology*, edited by Ernst Conradie, Sigurd Bergmann, Celia Deane-Drummond and Denis Edwards (London: Bloomsbury T&T Clark, 2014), 31–50.

pervasive and destructive though it is, fully captures the breadth and depth of the human predicament. In this context, it is worth noting that the Anthropocene narrative is not without ambiguity. One reading of it suggests that the answer to the crisis lies in even greater reliance on scientific and technological progress. If the problem is climate change, then should we not rely on science to diagnose the nature and extent of the problem and on technological progress to usher in a new economy driven by renewable sources of energy? What works for climate change is equally applicable to other environmental challenges. This approach rests essentially on the notion of human mastery over the environment, which is itself deeply problematic. Another reading of the Anthropocene presupposes that we may have already reached a tipping point, or that a series of tipping points are on the way and that remedial action is now too late. Such a reading can easily foreclose rather than open up possibilities for social action.

Grappling with the ecological emergency before us is without question critical to the human future. But much deeper reflection is called for, in theology as in the social sciences, if we are to devise appropriate responses to the emergency. The critical first step is to develop a multidimensional frame of analysis that can make sense of the current period of transition which signals the end of the Modern epoch, and of which the possible shift to a new geological age is but one, albeit dramatic, manifestation. To summarise in a few sentences an ambitiously interdisciplinary thesis elaborated in *Worlds in Transition*: human evolution, spanning some 150,000 years, has been characterised by a process of steady cultural and organisational complexification, though with considerable variations across time and space.[28] Important landmarks along the way include the development of language, agriculture (which coincides with the Holocene), writing, advanced metalworking (the Bronze Age), the rise of religious consciousness predicated on some kind of universalist vision or ethic (Axial Age), and the scientific, transportation, industrial and political revolutions which have given shape to the Modern Age.

All the indications are that, with Modernity having reached its intellectual and organisational limits, we are moving towards a new epoch marked by a paradigmatic shift in awareness and practice. We

---

28. Joseph A. Camilleri and Jim Falk, *Worlds in Transition: Evolving Governance across a Stressed Planet* (Cheltenham, UK: Edward Elgar, 2009).

may tentatively label this the *holoreflexive epoch* in that it represents, at least embryonically, a holistic response to the logic of exclusion. Holoreflexivity is planetary and ecocentric for it embraces the totality of relationships between the human species and the rest of the biosphere. But it is simultaneously global and human-centric in that it encompasses diverse nations, communities, cultures, religions and civilisations. Underlying its response to the challenges of a stressed and fractured world is the recognition that human destinies, generations past and future, all living things, matter and spirit are interconnected and interdependent. But it also acknowledges that the world is biologically and culturally plural. The holoreflexive shift is very much in its infancy, far from universal, and as yet hardly equal to the challenge, but it affirms inclusion as the defining feature of any viable approach to the ecology-peace nexus.

Religion's role in the roloreflexiveepoch

At this critical juncture in the human story, Christian eschatology cannot but be conscious of the immense destruction that humans have inflicted on each other and the planet and the many clouds that lurk on the horizon. It has to discern the signs of a 'groaning earth' (Rom 8:22–24). But this is not to validate capricious judgments unsupported by our present state of knowledge or an apocalyptic vision of the future that encourages despair and paralysis. Eschatology to have relevance for the human predicament must be transformational in the sense that action in the present is ethically informed by revisiting the past and reimagining the future. God, the divine presence in all things, has not abandoned the world, nor intends miraculous intervention. If relationships have to be reset and exclusionist tendencies are to be replaced by the ethos of inclusion, then responsibility lies firmly in human hands, both personally and institutionally. It is only in the context of the human being as steward, renovator and co-creator that the imagery of a new heaven and a new earth acquires its full meaning and content.

Religion's contribution, then, is to recognise the constraints of evolution, namely that the human species, like all other species, faces the prospect of extinction unless it is able to adapt continuously to a changing environment, a task made all the more difficult by past maladaptive choices that have ruptured both human relationships and ecosystems. But the call for adaptive and creative change goes beyond the imperatives of physical survival. Respect for the dignity of each person and for all life and recognition of the interdependence of all that exists in nature, respond to a subtler understanding of the workings of the Spirit. They are constitutive of a profound spirituality, one in which humans occupy a special place by virtue of the fact that they think, imagine, empathise, love and hope. In Boff's words, they have entered 'into the no longer instinctive but conscious phase of decision-making'.[29] As reflective beings they are embarked upon a journey which gives rise to a progressively more encompassing cosmology, or in Teilhard de Chardin's formulation, to the *noosphere* which grows towards ever greater integration and unification.[30] At this stage of the journey human beings are approaching holoreflexivity, with all the enhanced possibilities and responsibilities that this implies.

Religion, through its ritual practices, educational programs, community services, advocacy and other projects, is able not only to convey but to live this message. It thus becomes a potent agency for the formation of a higher consciousness and more inclusive ways of thinking, feeling, empathising, deciding and acting. This is precisely the intent of *Laudato Si'* as it is of other pronouncements and initiatives by such religious leaders as Ecumenical Patriarch Bartholomew, Dorothy Day, Martin Luther King, Thích Nhất Hạnh, Desmond Tutu and Oscar Romero. These are the prophetic voices that juxtapose in strikingly resonant ways the unacceptable present and the imagined future.

In the present conjuncture, the prophetic message needs to carry two interlinked and mutually reinforcing elements: ecological justice and a just peace. Boff offers the following formulation of the first element:

> Democracy must become socio-cosmic: that is, the elements of nature such as mountains, plants, rivers, animals and the atmosphere must be the new citizens who share in the human banquet, while humans share in the cosmic banquet.[31]

---

29. Boff, 'Liberation Theology and Ecology', 69
30. Pierre Teilhard de Chardin, *The Heart of Matter*, translated by René Hague (San Diego: Harcourt Brace & Co, 1978), 29–38.
31. Teilhard de Chardin, *The Heart of Matter*, 74.

The just peace element entails a re-commitment to the centrality of Gospel nonviolence. In line with this understanding a recent conference convened by the Pontifical Council for Justice and Peace and Pax Christi International called on the Catholic Church to:

- integrate Gospel nonviolence explicitly into the life, including the sacramental life, and work of the Church through dioceses, parishes, agencies, schools, universities, seminaries. . .
- promote nonviolent practices and strategies (e.g., nonviolent resistance, restorative justice, trauma healing, unarmed civilian protection, conflict transformation, and peace building . . .
- initiate a global conversation on nonviolence within the Church, with people of other faiths, and with the larger world . . .
- no longer use or teach 'just war theory'; continue advocating for the abolition of war . . .
- . . . challenge unjust world powers and to support and defend those . . . whose work for peace and justice puts their lives at risk.[32]

The interconnection of these two elements is clear enough. Regardless of the circumstances, all violence—physical, social and ecological—ultimately excludes, and thereby begets more violence.

The prophetic message alluded to above points to an ambitious agenda. It is especially daunting for religious institutions that have become heavily bureaucratised, fixated on institutional survival, and to a considerable extent infected by the prevailing spirit of exclusion and in difference. The task is made all the more difficult when those institutions present themselves as the ultimate repositories of truth. If religion is to rise to the immense challenge posed by the present historical moment, the major religious traditions, notwithstanding their diverse histories, belief systems and cultural expressions, have

---

32. 'An Appeal to the Catholic Church to Re-Commit to the Centrality of Gospel Nonviolence', Conference on Nonviolence and Just Peace: Contributing to the Catholic Understanding of and Commitment to Nonviolence, Rome, 11–13 April 2016, Pax Christi International <http://www.paxchristi.net/sites/default/files/documents/appeal-to-catholic-church-to-recommit-to-nonviolence.pdf>. Accessed 26 November 2016.

to acknowledge that none has a monopoly on wisdom and that each has unique insights and resources to contribute to a common endeavour of global and planetary dimensions.

The three Abrahamic faiths as well as Hinduism, Skikhism, Buddhism, to which we can add Confucianism and the Indigenous traditions (which though not strictly speaking religious have a strong 'spiritual' dimension), share a sense of the sacredness of all life, the dignity of the human person, a concern for standards of rightness in human conduct, and notions of respect and reverence that should guide humanity's relationship with both Earth and Heaven. These provide a sufficient common ground among these religious and ethical world views to make possible a wide-ranging and sustainable dialogue about human ethics in general and social-environmental ethics in particular.

For this purpose, agreement on doctrinal positions or authority structures is not required within, let alone between, these traditions. The aim rather should be to cultivate a dialogue of global proportions—global not so much in a geographic sense, but global in that it cultivates a 'global spirituality'. Such a dialogue is strategically placed to point to the transcendental, yet natural unity of the noosphere as well as the unity of all life. It needs to engage with and at the same time call into question the material unification of a consuming, not to say self-consuming, fragmenting and often violent world. This will be a dialogue that draws strength from both commonality and difference, and allows them to co-exist, illuminate and reinforce each other.

Two important dimensions of the dialogical process need particular attention. First, faith communities and their adherents face the difficult task of reconciliation. The history of each tradition right to the present time is steeped in the experience of suffering at the hands of others. Many religious minorities continue to endure the violence and humiliation to which others subject them. Yet, often these same communities are themselves the perpetrators of violence. Reconciliation therefore requires those in situations of tension and conflict to share their stories, listen to one another's experience of pain, acknowledge past wrongs, and accept responsibility for righting the wrongs of the past. It is this exercise in sustained mutual listening which is the basis for reconciliation and makes dialogue a force for healing.

All of the world's major religious and ethical traditions, each with its own distinctive history, ethos and symbolism, can contribute to the inclusiveness and universality of the holoreflexive epoch. In dialogue with each other their contribution is likely to prove more potent and efficacious. Such dialogue, when it does not limit itself to the beliefs of each tradition but encompasses the totality of their lived experience, is itself inclusivity at work. It opens up the possibility of a more holistic understanding of the human journey, establishing a closer connection between human needs and potentialities and between human rights and responsibilities. It helps cultivate a deeper sense of global engagement, where the individual person thinks and acts not as a disaggregated atom but as a member of several distinct yet overlapping and interacting communities, be it a community of faith, a local or national community, the international community, or the community of all living things. In the process, the prospect emerges of a deeper, evolving connection between humanity, Heaven and Earth.

Political Imaginings to Cultivate Eco-Lively Reflections on Violence

John McDowell

In a paper delivered as a conference plenary in September of 2015, the President of the Medical Association for the Prevention of War, Jenny Grounds, identified several crucial areas for moral concern and critical reflection. Two features were most prominent. First, the direct damage that war does to the environment. A visual display in an exhibition commemorating the centenary of the outbreak of the so-called 'Great War', the war that was supposed to end all wars, in the Melbourne Museum was poignant in this regard. Projected onto a large video screen was the image of a thriving forest which slowly began to turn into a series of images of eco-carnage in the form of trenches and mud. What was conspicuously missing from this latter scene, however, was the devastation not only of the environment but the slaughter of persons and animals.[1] Second was the indirect damage that results from costly investment in the industrial military complex and in continued warfare both of which distract from careful attention to ecological concerns and to the need for eco political flourishing. The cultivation of natality, to use Hannah Arendt's term, and biophilic mutuality, to use Rosemary Radford Ruether's, which take patience and care are promptly devastated during belligerent moments.[2]

---

1. Mentioning World War I was poignant given the timing of the conference two months shy of a century since the conference at Chantilly which planned the Allied strategy for 1916, and which resulted in the massive loss of human and animal life at Verdun and the Somme.
2. See Rosemary Radford Ruether on 'biophilic mutuality' in Michael S Northcott, *The Environment and Christian Ethics* (Cambridge: Cambridge University Press, 1996), 140.

I would like to build on these critical observations by pressing in a slightly different direction. My attention will be on what many commentators regard as the profound moral, spiritual and cultural crisis that underlies many of the problems we face. In this regard, ecology features as that which is affected by patterns of human behaviour, and therefore which demands a politics of ecologically significant performance. According to Michael Northcott, 'the loss of a spiritual account of the situatedness of the human self in a morally significant natural order is a central feature of the crisis we currently face'.[3]

Articulating what is here involved necessitates indicating the pathologies that manifest themselves in destructive behaviour, and which concomitantly refuse to face the absurdity of our regulative delusions. There is a deep and eminently practical need to circumvent the laziness of appeals to Manichaean rhetoric, with an attendant scapegoating mechanism that *alien* ates others and comforts the self through a 'politics of purity', and which exhibits itself in a form of moral insensitivity made adiaphorous by ideological conditioning. As Leonidas Donskis claims in conversation with Zygmunt Bauman, 'It turns out that a "healthy and normal person" can for a time turn into as much of a moral idiot as a sadistic sociopath'.[4] Susanne Kappeler makes a fine observation in this regard:

> War does not suddenly break out in a peaceful society .... The violence of our most commonsense everyday thinking, and especially our personal will to violence, constitute the conceptual preparation, the ideological armament and the intellectual mobilization which make the 'outbreak' of war ... of murder and destruction possible at all.[5]

---

3. Northcott, *The Environment and Christian Ethics*, 39. Cf. Rowan Williams, *Faith in the Public Square* (London: Bloomsbury, 2012), 196; Rudolf Bahro, *Avoiding Social and Ecological Disaster* (Bath: Gateway, 1994), 25; Timothy J Gorringe, *The Education of Desire: Towards a Theology of the Senses* (London: SCM, 2001); Peter Scott, *A Political Theology of Nature* (Cambridge: Cambridge University Press, 2003), 6.

4. Leonidas Donskis, in Zygmunt Bauman and Leonides Donskis, *Moral Blindness: The Loss of Sensitivity in Liquid Modernity* (Cambridge: Polity Press, 2013), 37.

5. Susanne Kappeler, *The Will to Violence: The Politics of Personal Behaviour* (Cambridge: Polity, 1995), 9. Cf. Peter De Angelis, 'The Logic of Violence: Foucault on How Power Kills', in *Philosophy and the Return of Violence: Studies from this Widening Gyre*, edited by Nathan Eckstrand and Christopher Yates (New York: Continuum, 2011), 172–88 (177).

In other words, beyond any description of current geopolitical and social arrangements, for issues concerning the biospheric impact of war, or for the relation of fratricide to ecocide, we need to produce a *genealogy* of war by identifying the ideological generation of what Grace Jantzen identifies as the 'death-drive' in the thanatised and necrophiliac imagination. This 'death-drive' is Jantzen's shorthand for a set of discursive practices that inhibits possibilities for promoting and realising flourishing in responsibly mutual relations. With a reference to Pierre Boudieu's concept of the *habitus*, she argues that the West is caught in the grip of 'a cultural fascination and obsession with death and violence, a preoccupation with death which is both dreaded and desired'.[6] Only in identifying 'this obsession with death which ... characterizes the habitus of western modernity', she contends, will the will to violent action (of which war is a species as an expression of a deathly *realpolitik*) be demythicised and therefore desacralised. In other words, echoing Kappeler's claim, Jantzen declares that 'it is not war, worrying though that is, upon which I think our attention should be focused'. Instead, she continues, 'war is no more than an explosive symptom of the systemic violence which spreads its underground tentacles throughout our cultural habitus'.[7] As Michel Foucault argues,

> those who resist or rebel against a form of power cannot merely be content to denounce violence .... What has to be questioned is the form of rationality at stake .... The question is: how are such relations of power rationalized?[8]

Therefore, he argues, 'The first methodological rule for this sort of work is ... to circumvent anthropological universals to the greatest extent possible, so as to interrogate them in their historical constitution'.[9] Jantzen, however, goes further than this. For her it

---

6. Grace M Jantzen, *Death and the Displacement of Beauty. Volume One: Foundations of Violence* (London: Routledge, 2004), 5. This sense of mutuality is crucial since as John Milbank laments, too much ecological reflection assumes that the value of humanity *should* decrease as nature increases; see John Milbank, *The Word Made Strange: Theology, Language, Culture* (Malden: Blackwell, 1997), 257–8.
7. Jantzen, *Foundations of Violence*, 29.
8. Michel Foucault, in *Michel Foucault: Power*, edited by James D Faubion (New York: The New Press, 2000), 324.
9. Foucault, cited in Jantzen, *Foundations of Violence*, 30.

is not sufficient merely to challenge and provoke, to destabilise the Western symbolic, since the critical challenge is to confront the collective loss of the capacity 'to imagine other sorts of response', what Rowan Williams calls 'Changing the myths we live by'.[10] Only then will the 'devastating consequences for humankind and the earth' be healed.[11]

In this vein I will refer as conceptual launching pads to three controlling literary images, somewhat broadly inspired by Richard Kearney's political use of the triad of strangers, monsters, and gods: Friedrich Nietzsche's madman from *The Gay Science*, Mary Shelley's *Frankenstein*, and the gardener as adapted from the image of the Dionysian garden in Euripides' *Bacchae*.[12] All coalesce around a conflictual ontology. The task is not to speak about war's ravaging impact on biospheric conditions; nor to stretch the bellicose image in a metaphorical fashion, environmental degradation as a 'war of terror on the natural world'. Rather, it is to handle both sets of issues together under Jantzen's than atological and natalising imagery in order to undertake a critical cultural politics for the reconfiguration of desire. Moreover I will speak of 'violence' rather than 'war' in order not to provide a euphemism that puts state or sovereign action at a dignified and masked remove from violence within states or sovereign territories, and therefore exempts *realpolitik* from moral critique. After all, as the Prussian Carl von Clausewitz famously claimed in 1832, 'war is the continuation of politics by other means'.[13] War, from an important perspective, is a version of gang violence ethically dressed up in the veneer of natural national virtue. It is profitable in this context, further, to resist the theologically naïve appeals to the 'just war' tradition when that reading is sundered from the contextual conditioning of it

---

10. Jantzen, *Foundations of Violence*, 29; Williams, *Faith in the Public Square*, 175.

11. Jantzen, *Foundations of Violence*, 5.

12. Richard Kearney, *Strangers, Monsters and Gods: Interpreting Otherness* (London: Routledge, 2003). Following Ulrich Beck, Henry A Giroux develops another image for the contemporary American political climate: that of the 'zombie': *Zombie Politics and Culture in the Age of Casino Capitalism* (New York: Peter Lang, 2011). The three imagistic categories I use here contain and relocate Giroux's most useful critical insights.

13. Carl von Clausewitz, *On War*, edited by Michael Howard and Peter Paret, (New Jersey: Princeton University Press, 1984), 87. *Der Kriegisteinebloße Fortsetzung der Politikmit anderen Mitteln.*

within a theology committed to the flourishing of all God's creatures in a covenantal ontology.

***

First, the madman.

In Nietzsche's narration of nihilism's origins, an acute contrast in attitudes is portrayed between the madman, who exclaims 'I seek God! I seek God!', and the derisively facetious crowd who lives on as if nothing has happened.[14] It is he alone who has grasped the significance of God's 'death' at humanity's hands. Thereby driven into the apprehensive insecurity of feeling set adrift with the cold night continually closing in, his terrified and anguished response becomes expressed by both his brief panic-stricken questions. What is more, it is from this predicament that the madman's questions take the form of providing highly suggestive apocalyptic allusions which startlingly eventuate in a sense that the 'sequence of breakdown, ruin, and cataclysm that is now impending' is for 'the whole of our European morality'.[15]

An apocalyptic image opens Alasdair MacIntyre's *After Virtue*.[16] In that text he argues forcefully that notions of the 'common good', of moral intuition, of shared moral understandings are no longer available to us with the fracturing of the ethical as a result of the dominance of nihilism, utilitarianism and emotivism. Moral deliberation either reduces agents to calculable entities, 'a mere statistical unit' in a moral calculus, or to those engaging in the indeterminacy of 'choice' as agents become ontologically 'minimal' (Christopher Lasch) or 'liquid' (Zygmunt Bauman) selves.[17] From this it becomes crucial to ask how far our ethical reflections on war and ecology endure as if nothing has happened, as if a shared moral framework can continue to direct our deliberations.

One form that such a question can take is whether we continue to speak glibly of an ethics of the 'just war' as if contemporary bellicos-

---

14. Friedrich Nietzsche, *The Gay Science*, translated Walter Kaufmann (New York: Vintage Books, 1974), 125.
15. Nietzsche, *The Gay Science*, 343.
16. Alasdair MacIntyre, *After Virtue: A Study in Moral Theory*, second edition (Notre Dame: University of Notre Dame Press, 1984), 1–2.
17. Citation from Donskis, in *Moral Blindness*, 52.

ity remains in the hands of clearly definable sovereign states; and as if these states can now offer 'cleaner' kills with advanced precision technologies; and as if we do not now have at our command weapons of such destructive potency that there becomes no-one in range who, to all intents and purposes, does not become a casualty even if a non-combatant.

A further dimension of the question has to do with the way much ecological and also ecospiritual reflection operates. Such reflections often emerge as post-Romantic responses to a supposed pre-linguistic 'experience' of things. As a consequence, they have more in common with Kant's sublime, and they are hampered by similar difficulties such as the pre-linguistic notion of 'experience', the essentialist singularity of this notion of 'experience', the bourgeois appeal to the aesthetic wherein the aesthetic sensibility is scythed from ethical significance, and the consequent subjectivisation of the moral reference. This involves a quite distinctive moral ontology founded on a reconfiguration of the relations of body and mind, the self and others, and human beings to nature. The Good is reduced to the Beautiful, at least when the aesthetic is sublimated or *made sublime*. The question needs to be asked what ecospirituality and religiously informed ecological responsibility must look like when they are more adequately critically attuned to the difficulties of cultural solipsism that attend constructivist anthropologies intensively reflective of Kant's category of 'spontaneity'. What must they become if they are to be critically freed from a colonising transcendentalist paradigm, what Terry Eagleton refers to as an 'authoritarianism of intuition', a 'lethal ecstasy'?[18]

The image of the madman, and perhaps the stranger as madman so that all becomes 'other', is not in and of itself a violently colonising move. Its conditions at most inhibit biospheric flourishing from its regulating perspective of transcendental sublimity. The step into violence, instead, requires a further move, the making the other *monstrous.*

∗∗∗

---

18. Terry Eagleton, *Holy Terror* (Oxford: Oxford University Press, 2005), 3, 13. Milbank regards the ecofeminism of Sally McFague to be reducible to a 'Green leisure theology' (263). Milbank sarcastically defines this as a theology 'enabling the self to communicate with the cosmos in time off from work.'

If the first image was that of the madman, then the second, that of Mary Shelley's narrative of monstrosity from 1818, might seem at first to be at a far remove. However, some of the work that this second concept can do might well be prepared for by referring to Terry Gilliam's dystopian *12 Monkeys*. In a Foucaultian move, one of the characters Jeffrey Goines announces in an asylum to the main protagonist James Cole,

> … we're consumers. Buy a lot of stuff and you're a good
> citizen. But if you don't buy a lot of stuff … what are you then
> I ask you, what? Mentally ill.

This is echoed later in the drama by Dr Peters who asks rhetorically 'isn't it obvious that … homo sapiens' motto "let's go shopping" is the cry of the true lunatic?'

As Elaine Graham observes, '*Frankenstein* stands as one of the quintessential representations of the fears and hopes engendered by new technologies'.[19] However, while Victor Frankenstein's reanimated product is often referred to as 'Frankenstein's monster', the book actually suggests something quite different. The subtlety in Shelley's raising of the issue of the monstrous in a distinctive fashion was distinctly lost to the Hollywood of 1910 and even more famously James Whale's movie of 1931. Since its Hollywoodisation Shelley's story has largely been pitched as a horror played out for cheap and momentary thrills. The back cover of my own copy of the novel published by Arrow Books carries the description: 'The most sinister, blood-curdling horror story of all time'. Admittedly Shelley writes,

> I busied myself *to think of a story*—a story to rival those which
> had excited us to this task. One which would speak to the
> mysterious fears of our nature and awaken thrilling horror—
> one to make the reader dread to look round, and curdle the
> blood, and quicken the beatings of the heart.[20]

---

19. Elaine L Graham, *Representations of the Post/Human* (Manchester: Manchester University Press, 2002), 62.

20. Mary Shelley, *Frankenstein or, the Modern* Prometheus (London: Arrow Books, 1973), 8.

Yet, as Elaine Graham rightly maintains, 'monstrosity, for so long automatically assigned to the creature, may need to be distributed in different directions altogether'.[21] That means that the work is considerably richer and more chilling in a dystopian fashion than contemporary understandings of it as horror would suggest.

It is often assumed that the issue of the book is one of the self-destructiveness of 'playing god', and therefore of the modern Prometheus' *hubris* that comes with attempting things that only God alone should do.[22] This is the type of argument that often appears in criticisms of new technologies such as cloning. Shelley herself makes a suggestion to this effect in her 'Author's Introduction': 'supremely frightful would be the effect of any human endeavour to mock the stupendous mechanism of the Creator of the world.'[23] However, that would not make sense of her Romanticism, her participation in a cultural ethos that has to do with the movement of the human spirit in and through aesthetic creativity. Rather, the dramatically central theme of the book has to do with the intellectual sensibility that separates scientific inquiry from moral responsibility. Dr Frankenstein is consumed by the desire to prove his theories of reanimation, a desire that comes to determine all of his other attitudes and actions. As a consequence of that single-mindedness, the story becomes one of tragedy and catastrophe. Not only does he lose all that he professes to love, but the construction of his scientific labours erupts violently against him.

Shelley's novel does not provide some glib cautionary tale about overreaching forms of scientific knowledge or creativity. Instead, its caution occurs dramatically in its move into becoming a tragedy. The mirror is held up to movements of the human spirit informing it of the horror of its desires, desires for knowledge disconnected from moral responsibility. As she articulates, the book 'affords a point of view to the imagination for the delineating of human passions' and their destructiveness under certain conditions. Unhindered by sufficient trepidation and anti-hubristic modesty, Victor's tragic flaw, then, is not the discovery of the science of reanimation, but rather his instrumentalisation of life. After all, the so-called 'monster' is

---

21. Graham, *Representations of the Post/Human*, 63.
22. See Daniel Dinello, *Technophobia! Science Fiction Visions of Posthuman Technology* (Austin: University of Texas Press, 2005), 41.
23. Shelley, *Frankenstein*, 9.

not even given a name, a signal of 'a deeply enigmatic quality: a lack of definitive identity'.[24] Even the theft of body parts that are spliced together into a grotesque figure provides the sense of a butcher working with dead flesh. The 'monster', so-called, is not reanimated in order to be human, but in order to be an object and mere instrument of Victor's 'obsessive attempt to cheat death and to place humanity in a position of mastery and domination over non-human nature'.[25] In that regard, the story provides a critical investigative penetration into the destructively inhuman possibilities of 'irresponsible knowing'.[26] It is the fruit of this which generates the conditions for the violence that overflows Victor's control, and sweeps him agonisingly up in its deadly grip. His ambitions pay no heed to the well-being of others, as the one designated as 'monster' laments towards the end of a lavish and sophisticated speech expressing awe and wonder over the magnificence of nature in contrast to his discovery of the beastly brutality and violent in hospitality of human beings.[27] That is why, as Graham observes, 'Shelley's focus on Victor's personality was central to her depiction of the disastrous implications of his flawed scientific method'.[28] In that regard, the novel disturbs the sense of who the reader thinks the monster is. The monster is less the product of Frankenstein's hands than the typing of the scientist himself. Jantzen rhetorically asks, 'Who is mad and who is sane in a world in which beauty confronts death, and violence silences creativity?'[29] *Frankenstein* encourages us to ask something similar about the monstrous.

Shelley's startling tale indicates something of the early modern shifts in the understanding of human agency as they are formed by a new framing of subjectivity and the objectivisation of that which is to be known and acted on, and of the political as the venue, as Thomas Hobbes declared, for controlling the natural war of all against all. It is here in the mechanised metaphysics of, the universal regulation by,

---

24. Graham, *Representations of the Post/Human*, 64.

25. Graham, *Representations of the Post/Human*, 64.

26. Graham, *Representations of the Post/Human*, 82.

27. See Slavoj Žižek, *Violence: Six Sideways Reflections* (London: Profile Books, 2008), 39; Graham, *Representations of the Post/Human*, 64, 66.

28. Graham, *Representations of the Post/Human*, 75.

29. Jantzen, *Foundations of Violence*, 3. Jantzen uses psychoanalytic discourse of neuroses and therapy to describe many of the aspects regulating modern Western society and the need for a healing redemption (*Foundations of Violence*, 4).

the rationalising and objectivising spirit that what Martin Heidegger calls the 'technological age' or Herbert Marcusse names the 'universe of instrumentalities' is born.[30] As Graham argues,

> Victor's obsessive interest, framed in the language of quest and objectification, thus closely reflects an instrumental approach to knowledge, reminiscent of Bacon's notorious coupling of scientific understanding with the conquest of inanimate nature.[31]

It is, therefore, both deeply poignant and significant that Jürgen Moltmann regards modernity's conception as occurring in the colonialism of 1492, and its othering of the Other who now becomes an 'alien' to be either resisted or calculably used out of self-interest.[32] The universe is thereby emptied of value, significance, purpose and the situatedness of action as ethically responsible. Accordingly, the classical liberal notion of justice gives systematic preference to the view of life in which 'human dignity consists in autonomy, that is, in the ability of each person to determine for himself or herself a view of the good life'.[33] Herein lies what we might refer to from Max Weber as 'the disenchantment of the world' or in Peter Scott's terms as the *disgracing of creation*, a 'Displacement towards nature [which] was … in place from the outset of modernity'.[34] In this context,

---

30. Herbert Marcusse, *One Dimensional Man* (Boston, 1964), 235. Jürgen Habermas: 'Rationalization [for Max Weber] means, first of all, the extension of the areas of society subject to the criteria of rational decision. Second, social labor is industrialized, with the result that the criteria of instrumental action also penetrates into other areas of life (urbanization of the mode of life, technification of transport and communication).' See *Toward a Rational Society: Student Protest, Science, and Politics*, translated by Jeremy J Shapiro (London: Heinemann Educational Books, 1971), 81.

31. Graham, *Representations of the Post/Human*, 76.

32. Jürgen Moltmann, *God for a Secular Society: The Public Relevance of Theology*, translated by Margaret Kohl (Minneapolis: Fortress Press, 1999), 6. Rosemary Radford Ruether criticises the abusive domination and destructive oppression of nature through technology as a symptom what she identifies as the male tendency to dominate and control; see *Gaia and God: An Ecofeminist Theology of Earth Healing* (London: SCM, 1993), 2.

33. Charles Taylor, cited in Miroslav Volf, *Exclusion and Embrace: A Theological Exploration of Identity, Otherness, and Reconciliation* (Nashville: Abingdon Press, 1996), 201.

34. Scott, *A Political Theology of Nature*, 8; citation from Milbank, *The Word Made Strange*, 258.

> Any secreted knowledge could now be deployed on behalf of power, and knowledge defined as prying is none other than the power of vision to survey its objects with impunity (however much, through the dialectics of the gaze, such impunity may prove to be an illusion).[35]

The teleological logics of knowing are evacuated and replaced by a procedural logic of pure will and the technical competency of potential for that will to be omnipotent. So Eagleton argues that 'The omnipotent will which bullies Nature to do its bidding is another name for absolute freedom'.[36] Accordingly, it appears that

> the rise of instrumental views of nature has gone hand in hand with the demise of the traditional Christian view of creation as the sphere of God's providential ordering, and with the gradual secularisation of European civilisation which began at the close of the Middle Ages and reaches its nadir in secularised modernity.[37]

That means that we should all now be over and past Lynn White's historically and theologically shallow and intellectually lazy critique of the roots of the environmental crisis.[38] As Brad Evans and Henry Giroux admit, 'The utopian promise of the Enlightenment thus contained within it the violence and brutalities embedded in the logic of instrumental rationality', and therefore 'the unchecked appeal to progress and ideological purity'.[39]

Moreover, this instrumentalising move has gone hand in hand with what Theodor Adorno laments about 'mass culture'—the trivialisation of the cultural by consumerist values of profit and distracting consumption.[40] It is here that what Deleuzian inspired Daniel Bell calls the capitalist technology of desire emerges and spreads in the

---

35. Milbank, *The Word Made Strange*, 258.
36. Eagleton, *Holy Terror*, 104.
37. Northcott, *The Environment and Christian Ethics*, 83–4.
38. Lynn White, 'The Historical Roots of Our Environmental Crisis', in *Science* 155 (1967), 1203–7.
39. Brad Evans and Henry A Giroux, *Disposable Futures: The Seduction of Violence in the Age of Spectacle* (San Francisco: City Lights Books, 2015), 13.
40. Theodor Adorno, *The Culture Industry: Selected Essays on Mass Culture*, edited by JM Bernstein (London: Routledge, 1991).

violent, competitive and instrumentalising form of 'savage capitalism' that is sustained by 'cancerous consumption', and is reducible to the self-perpetuating nihilism of ungrounded desire.[41] Such a move results in state terror, the terror of the market advancing military invasion; of quelling dissent at home; and of the market's 'disposable lives'. Accordingly, Slavoj Žižek indicates in his reflections on the aftermath of the catastrophe in New Orleans, that we have to recognise the reduction of meaning 'generated by capitalist dynamics' to 'individualist competition', a teleology shaped around only the desires of the individual, survivalist struggle of the fittest, and 'ruthless self-assertion' that is 'much more threatening and violent than all the hurricanes and earthquakes'.[42]

A further layer to this is the development in capitalist societies of the 'entertainment culture', and this has at least three significant overlaps with this essay's interests: firstly, the forms of distraction from critique, ethical responsibility, and even the outrage that fuels revolution that result from what Adorno regarded as the newly intensified sigh of the oppressed masses, the amusing of ourselves to death (Neil Postman), the emergence of us as Nietzschean Last Men.[43] Secondly, the translation of violence into a satisfying spectacle, into *militainment*, and the underlying agonistic ontology that ideologically naturalises this violent spectacle. As Jantzen argues, 'Violence has so colonized our habitus that we have collectively lost the capacity to imagine other sorts of response.'[44] This is a conceptually more interesting claim than those dogging disputes about 'copycat' violence. Donskis displays well what, among other things, is at stake:

> The routinization of violence and killing during war leads to
> a condition in which people stop responding to war's horrors.
> … constant stimuli force people to cease reacting to them.[45]

---

41. Daniel M Bell, Jr, *Liberation Theology After the End of History: The Refusal to Cease Suffering* (London: Routledge, 2001), 10, 85. The concept of 'savage capitalism' is developed by Bell from Franz Hinkelammert. Cf. Bell, *The Economy of Desire: Christianity and Capitalism in a Postmodern World* (Grand Rapids.: Baker Academic, 2012).

42. Žižek, *Violence*, 82.

43. On Nietzsche's criticism of the Last Man, see Žižek, *Violence*, 24–5.

44. Jantzen, *Foundations of Violence*, 27.

45. Donskis, in *Moral Blindness*, 37.

Third, given the increasing scarcity of certain resources, such as fossil fuels, crucial for the profitable functioning of Western economies:

> How supplies are to be secured at existing levels becomes a grave political and moral question for the wealthier states, and a real destabilizer of international relations. This is a situation with all the ingredients for the most vicious kinds of global conflict – conflict now ever more likely to be intensified by the tensions around religious and cultural questions.[46]

All in all, 'We live at a time in which instrumental rationality', particularly well expressed in the biopolitics of the 'free' market, 'appears increasingly divorced from the community-building values of democracy, public life, and education.'[47] And this is all advanced in the name of progress. Yet, as Adorno warns in critique of glib talk of modern progress,

> It would be advisable to think of progress in the crudest, most basic terms: that no one should go hungry anymore, that there should be no more torture, no more Auschwitz. Only then will the idea of progress be free from lies.[48]

****

Third, and finally, the garden.

According to Charles Taylor, 'the refusal to define any goods other than … instrumental efficiency in the search for happiness can lead to appalling destruction in a society's way of life.'[49] Such instrumentalisation accords with Jantzen's critique of thanatological impulses permeating and informing the moral imagination in the West. In an early theological study, she makes it clear that she finds dualistic philosophy of Cartesianism, originating in many ways in the Platonic

---

46. Williams, *Faith in the Public Square*, 180.

47. Evans and Giroux, *Disposable Futures*, 63.

48. Theodor Adorno, cited by Detlev Claussen, *Theodor W Adorno: One Last Genius* (Cambridge, MA: Harvard University Press, 2008), 338.

49. Charles Taylor, *Sources of the Self: The Making of Modern Identity* (Cambridge: Cambridge University Press, 1989), 340. Northcott: 'The anti-relational economic ethic of the pursuit of self-interest, and the rationalist ethic of utilitarian individualism both ignore this relationality in the structure of life on earth.' Northcott, *The Environment and Christian Ethics*, 121.

privileging of mind, particularly unconvincing.[50] So much so that she claims that 'an unbridled lust for technological power … [derives from a particular root]: a rift between the material world and spiritual value'.[51] Her interests in overcoming this binary by more adequately imagining the nature of the commerce between God and creature lead her to promote the image of the world as 'God's body', and this, she claims, provides some critical practical advantages: 'The model of the universe as God's body helps to do justice to the beauty and value of nature, the importance of conservation and ecological responsibility, the significance and dignity of the human body and human sexuality.'

However, even at its best, it remains a model that is, like all theological models distinctly limited. For instance, it does not cope particularly well with the notion of creation as the product of pure divine gratuity, since persons do not give themselves their bodies. Moreover, despite some sterling efforts on Jantzen's part, it is not well equipped to ensure either that God and world do not fold into one another, thereby endangering the integrity of creaturely life as an autonomous-life-in-dependence-on-divine beneficence, or preventing the naturalising of suffering. Is monism any less a theological projection than is dualism, and therefore does it sufficiently do justice to the constant hesitations of the apophatic tradition? At worst, this *choosing* to operate by a different regulating metaphor emerges as a form of what Milbank calls 'crypto-fascism': that is, a form of thought that is deluded in imagining that it can know what the common good looks like from which to generate supportive theological models, but operates as an act of arbitrary self-assertion on the part of desire.[52] As William Placher warns,

> Functionalism [in theological imagining] opens the door to idolatry, and the dominant idols are, in the end, those of the powerful. If we let human beings design God, then the socially dominant result will not be a deity fitted to the needs of the oppressed of the world.[53]

---

50. Grace M Jantzen, *God's World, God's Body* (London: Darton, Longman and Todd, 1984).
51. Jantzen, *God's World*, 156.
52. Milbank, *The Word Made Strange*, 262. For Milbank's critique of McFague, see 263ff., especially the criticism of McFague's weak appeal to God's 'sympathising' with God's body.
53. William C Placher, *The Domestication of Transcendence: How Modern Thinking About God Went Wrong* (Louisville: Westminster John Knox Press, 1996), 16.

The result is a form of value and meaning constructed by the will and this is well suited to the 'free' marketplace. However, in *Becoming Divine* Jantzen develops a different image in response to instrumentalising desire: the natalising garden. By 'natality' she explains:

> the fact that we were born, that we are all 'natals'—against the fact that we shall all die, that we are all 'mortals'. … it is in birth, in natality, that newness enters into the world; and it is in the fact of new life that every other form of freedom and creativity is grounded, a creativity that is contrary to violence and destruction. If natality is ignored in an obsession with death and violence, it is small wonder that the world hovers on the brink of destruction.[54]

Accordingly, weaning the neurotic cultural imagination off its nihilistic obsession with death and violence involves envisioning resources for the disciplining of desire—specifically the shaping of responsive action and hope—through, Jantzen advocates, a creative 'poetics of natality'.[55]

One of several texts she appeals to is Hosea 14:3–7 in which comes the divine promise that Israel 'shall flourish as a garden' and 'shall blossom like the vine'.[56] These reflections demand the fullness of the bodying forth of an habituated ethic of mutuality for the abundant symbiotic flourishing of life together, in contradistinction to the various 'nay-sayings' to life that she detects in Christian soteriology, especially as it has been reanimated by Cartesian subjectivity. To this we should add the Christian reimagining of the teleological in the form of an apocalyptic catastrophism.[57]

Cultivating the life-giving metaphor of natality stimulates a number of creative possibilities, must noticeably including a privileging of 'embodiment. To be born is to be embodied, enfleshed.'[58] Moreover,

---

54. Jantzen, *Foundations of Violence*, 6.

55. Jantzen, *Foundations of Violence*, 35.

56. Citations from *Hosea* 14:7 nrsv. See Grace M. Jantzen, *Becoming Divine: Towards a Feminist Philosophy of Religion* (Manchester: Manchester University Press, 1998), 157.

57. Jantzen is aware of the way in which a focus on 'some *other* world, [leads inevitably] away from the flourishing of the whole person in *this* world' (*Foundations of Violence*, 36). However, her argument would be strengthened further by locating the violence at the heart of numerous apocalyptic accounts of the eschatological.

58. Jantzen, *Foundations of Violence*, 36.

this image of materiality is one of interdependent relationality and the mutuality of justice, and even of the sensuousness of touch involved in horticultural tactility.[59] Thereby it upsets the predominance of individualised soteriological notions and the political significance of the Hobbesian imagery of flourishing by oneself, as well as the adversarial construing of relations in predominantly competitive terms, leading to the disposability of others' lives.[60]

> It is possible to die alone, but it is not possible to be born alone: there must be at least one other person present, and she, in turn, was born of someone else. To be natal means to be part of a web of relationships, both diachronous and synchronous: it means, negatively, that atomistic individualism is not possible for natals.[61]

But more than this, the cultivation image can advocate a shift in the symbolic from a social imaginary of desire's rapacious utilisation to one of symbiotic flourishing in responsible and co-operative care and tending to the wellbeing of 'the other' (as long, of course, as the horticultural metaphor is conditioned by more than the therapeutic forms gardening well suited to a privatised culture). In this regard, Graham believes that 'An ethic of "natality" helps to expose', for instance, Victor Frankenstein's 'dysfunctional and necrophilic impulses'. Moreover, 'it should also assist in expanding predominant understandings of what it means to be human, a process which the creature's own testimony seems to demand'.[62]

And yet the question remains, of course, on what soil can this flourishing be cultivated, and in what form does the theological appeal come? After all, the garden can be a site of suffering and destruction, not only in Gethsemane but in Euripides' *The Bacchae*, a text whose Dionysian exuberance so caught Nietzsche's imagination as to ground his early Schopenhauerian tragic agonism. In the Euripedean material, the garden comes to signal a chaotic and uncontrollable delight,

---

59. On the importance of touch and embrace, see, for example, Luce Irigaray, *To Be Two*, translated by Monique Rhodes and Marco Cocito-Monoc (London: The Athlone Press, 2000), 25.
60. See Jantzen, *Becoming Divine*, 164.
61. Jantzen, *Foundations of Violence*, 37.
62. Graham, *Representations of the Post/Human*, 83.

a bodying forth of desires that are violently irresponsible for civic life. In this regard, the cultivation metaphor serves to perpetuate the individuation of desire unconstrained by conditions that might otherwise be politically perceived as being socially demanding of the range of responsibility. Liberating conditions are not well serviced by the arbitrary imaginative reconstructions of meaning, and their free floating function rooted only in a metaphysics of self-expansive but reactive desire, echoing the political turn of the Romantic move into sublimity. From whence grows the conditions of plenitude beyond a scarcity that is conducive to cutthroat competition and its justification in an ideology of sacrifice, of giving beyond grasping, of other-serving hospitality beyond the other-using exclusion of self-aggrandising self-assertion? What Jantzen's own analysis of 'natality' is moving towards is an account of the poietic metaphysics of the plenitudinous *gift*, and it is only here that non-arbitrary forms of healing the human imagination from the pathologies of violence can *ontologically* take place and cultivate an ecopolitically responsible performance in hope. Herein is a vital set of resources for the habituating realisation of 'the interconnectedness of all things and their dependence on what we cannot finally master'.[63]

---

63. Williams, *Faith in the Public Square*, 193.

Our War with Nature and Each Other from a Buddhist Perspective: Insights from Buddhism and Sharon Welch

Shelini Harris

In this essay, I argue that the reasoning that considers war, especially the more devastating forms of modern warfare, to be a solution to conflicts between human societies, is also responsible for our war with nature. Such thinking, rooted in a lack of recognition of the interrelatedness of all life, has culminated in the dominance of an ethic of control governing the relationship between humans and the rest of nature. Because we are all interrelated, any action taken on others ultimately has consequences for ourselves, and precludes absolute control over the actions of others and certainty of outcome. I illustrate how this approach has dominated not only relations between humans and nations, but also our relationship with nature.

As Sharon Welch argues, responsible action has come to be defined in terms of being able to exert a significant amount of control and concomitant assurance of very specific outcomes; which is unrealistic given the complexity and interrelatedness of social and natural processes. I show how such modes of thinking and acting in affairs relating to humans and the rest of nature have resulted in disastrous consequences. Using some examples from Buddhism and other contexts, I illustrate how a world view based on the inter connectedness of all life leads people to take into consideration the lifestyles and needs of other parties, assuming a degree of mutual responsibility with its associated risks. While this option may seem too risky and full of uncertainties, I argue that in the long run, it has fewer devastating consequences than our current modes of operation based on an ethic of control as responsibility. Buddhist approaches have a lot to contribute in thinking about alternatives that acknowledge vulnerability, embrace mutuality and an ethic of risk, which seek to open matrices of possibilities rather than unilaterally predetermined ends. The tendency to go to war and the desire to control are not uniquely modern; what is modern is the attempt to apply this mode of operation across most aspects of life and surroundings; no doubt facilitated and inspired by the scientific discoveries and construction of the nation-states, with the emphasis on subjecting more and more aspects of life to centralised state control. And most significantly, violence and war are defined in moral terms as responsible action—not just self-defence but universal humanitarianism. As such, my focus is not so much on our greed, vice and general actions of ill will, but in how we seek to do good.

The ethic of control and separation

One of the most unfortunate founding ideologies shaping modern civilisation regarding responsible action argues that the safest and best way of organising societies is to ensure we have control of every aspect of our lives, having the ability to foresee and control the outcomes. In fact, this was the measure of human advancement in the drive towards progress. The most influential development theories differentiated traditional societies (in need of development) from modern ones in terms of the degree to which they exhibited centralised organisational and political control over their regions, exerting control over their natural surroundings (considered to be separate from humans) for production purposes.[1] The most efficient and progressive way to

---

1. For instance, in the last century, Samuel Huntington, an influential political scientist, points out that the difference between traditional societies and modern ones is that in the former people were 'passive and acquiescent', conceiving themselves as continuous with nature and not exerting control over their environment, especially for production processes. Samuel Huntington, 'The Change to Change: Modernization, Development, and Politics (1971)', in *From Modernization to Globalization: Perspectives on Development and Social Change*, edited by J Timmons Roberts and Amy Hite (Oxford: Blackwell, 2000), 145. Walt Rostow also noted that while traditional societies did have some form of central power in their political organisations, the regions were far more self-sufficient and had more power than in the modern structures, which means that centralised organisational control would be weak. Walt W Rostow, 'Stages of Economic Growth: A Non-Communist Manifesto (1960)', in *From Modernization to Globalization: Perspectives on Development and Social Change*, edited by J Timmons Roberts and Amy Hite (Oxford: Blackwell, 2000), 100. This

organise and run societies was assumed to be through centralised control based on standardised prescriptions applied universally. These assumptions were based on the authority of science and evolutionary theories, positing the notion of linear development patterned on the path of European societies, considered to be at the advanced stages of what was the universal unfolding of the progress of societies. On this basis other societies were subjected to drastic transformation of their values, ways of life, and especially, their relationship with nature.

As James Scott points out, this effort to control all aspects of life has led to zoning, forestry and regulations affecting minute details of life, allowing the state or authorities to monitor more and more aspects of life, either to deliver services (much of it delineated in human rights) or for surveillance.[2] As he explains, this entails categorisation and simplification of humans, societies and the rest of nature, including their activities and processes, and reorganising landscapes and social structures, all to better facilitate control from outside in a top-down manner.[3] He points out that high modernism functions like a faith, though based on the authority and legitimacy of science and technology. It has a level of uncritical optimism about the degree of knowledge and certainty that can be gained about human societies and natural processes that is unscientific.[4] For instance, even in the field of international law, Anne Orford describes how the belief in the universality and objectivity of the scientific method was taken to be applicable to the legal science, which was then deemed capable of arriving at universal principles found in all legal systems, facilitating the codification of knowledge.[5] Such assumptions facilitate the kind of policies and interventions discussed below.

---

was seen as the weakness of 'traditional' societies by proponents of the dominant model of development and modernisation. This is the exact opposite of what is called for by those advocating the construction of more sustainable and self-sufficient societies as we face issues like climate change, global financial crises and other problems.

2. James C Scott, *Seeing Like a State: How Certain Schemes to Improve the Human Condition Have Failed* (New Haven: Yale University Press, 1998), 2. Scott discusses various aspects of the negative consequence of the effort to improve human life by ever increasing processes of control.
3. Scott, *Seeing,* 191.
4. Scott, *Seeing,* 4.
5. Anne Orford, 'Scientific Reason and the Discipline of International Law', in *The European Journal of International Law,* 25/2 (2014): 373, 378.

Implications for war in human society

In a world of unequal power, the penchant for control coupled with the justification of violence on the grounds of compassion leads to dire consequences which are apparent today. Talal Asad asserts that 'the exercise of violence is intrinsic to the modern concept of the human'.[6] He traces a tendency within the history of Christianity which considers the use of violence as compatible with love.[7] He says, 'The mutual embrace of compassion and violence is thus central to this concept of humanity, and it continues as a strand in post-Christian military humanitarianism…'.[8] Ethicist Sharon Welch observes:

> Part of the twist at the heart of the Western concept of goodness is the very construction of responsible action, an atomistic understanding of the moral actor. These false abstractions mask a fundamental disrespect for other individuals and nations that poisons attempts to do good. It is not accidental that such confidence in the superiority of one's moral vision is accompanied by plans to coerce others, and leaves one dissatisfied with attempts to persuade them to comply with a certain course of action. The certainty of rightness does not lead to a desire to dialogue with others about their visions of rightness or about possible strategies to reach those visions because it is accompanied by a fundamental disdain for the views of others. It is extremely difficult for this disrespect to be seen, for it wears the face of moral responsibility.[9]

Furthermore, in discussing the causes of war and the nuclear arms race, she says that this too has to do with the mistaken notions about

---

6.   Talal Asad, 'Reflections on Violence, Law, and Humanitarianism', in *Critical Inquiry*, 41/2 (2015): 390–427, 403.

7.   Asad is primarily concerned with the modern form of humanitarianism evident in international law and morality, which embraces a paradoxical approach of quelling violence with violence, a tendency apparent since St. Augustine who declared that punishment should be carried out in love. As he points out, even the crusades were imbued with the notion of love: see discussion, Asad, 'Reflections on Violence', 393–7.

8.   Asad, 'Reflections on Violence', 397–8.

9.   Sharon D Welch, *A Feminist Ethic of Risk* (Minneapolis: Fortress Press, 1990), 41.

security and responsible action, based on an immoral balance of power.[10] She observes:

> The only type of power that is guaranteed to be successful is destructive power. One can ensure the death of an enemy, but one cannot ensure the cooperation of another in mutually fulfilling transforming work. The pursuit of guaranteed total fulfilment produces the destruction of life.[11]

As Simone Weil argues:

> When two human beings have to settle something and neither has the power to impose anything on the other, they have to come to an understanding. Then justice is consulted, for justice alone has the power to make two wills coincide. But when there is a strong and a weak there is no need to unite their will. There is only one will, that of the strong. The weak obeys. Everything happens just as it does when a man is handling matter. There are not two wills to be made to coincide… Beyond a certain degree of inequality in the relations of men of unequal strength, the weaker passes into the state of matter and loses his personality.[12]

Given the stark levels of inequality between and within nations, Weil's insight indicates what could happen even in seemingly multilateral decision-making processes 'motivated by humanitarianism'.[13] Ecolog-

---

10. As she argues, only those who are privileged and are used to having such levels of power over others would conceive of responsible action in terms of being able to have absolute control (after all, that is what nuclear weapons are about) over one's opponent and the possible outcome.
11. Welch, *Feminist Ethic,* 120.
12. Simone Weil, *Waiting for God* (New York: Putnam's Sons, 1951), 142.
13. Even those within the field of dominant economics have raised some concerns regarding the level of inequality and its implications for the well-being of the poor. For instance, Martin Ravallion, a former Director of the World Bank's research department, the Development Research Group, discussed this in 'Global Inequality: Are the Poorest Being Left Behind?' (paper presented at Crawford School of Economics, Australian National University, 9 June 2015). Also, Guanghua Wan 'Poverty in Asia: A Deeper Look' (paper presented at Crawford School of Economics, Australian National University, 28 August 2014). Wan is Principal Economist and Head of Poverty-Inequality Research Group, the Asian Development Bank. Previously, he was Senior Economist in the United Nations.

ical economists are also concerned that inequality is an impediment to the fostering of communities where in mutual decisions necessary for addressing climate change can be made.[14] While pointing out that the United States is not the only country with this kind of power, Rob Nixon says that since World War II it 'has wielded an unequalled power to bend the global regulatory climate in its favour.'[15]

The historically accumulated degree of inequality between peoples and almost concomitant power over and separation from nature has driven us down this current path of warfare. It is not that earlier societies living more in continuity with nature did not go to war, but that modern wars are not parsed as two nations going to war over resources or other disputes as was the case in the past. Our modern discourse allows us to describe the invasion of other nations, the complete overthrow of their systems, and horrific bombings, all as the 'responsibility to protect', as in the recent declaration by the United Nations and global authorities.[16] International lawyer Anne Orford points out that '…grounding authority on the capacity to protect has historically tended to privilege certain kinds of institutions and certain forms of action over others. The turn to protection focuses upon creating institutions that privilege coherence, control, and centralisation.'[17] Orford observes that this raises the question of who

---

14. Robert Costanza *et al.*, 'Building a Sustainable and Desirable Economy-in-Society-in-Nature', in *State of the World 2013: Is Sustainability Still Possible?* (Worldwatch Institute), 134.

15. Rob Nixon, *Slow Violence and the Environmentalism of the Poor* (Cambridge: Harvard University Press, 2011), 36.

16. Beginning in the 1990s, following the conflicts in Rwanda and the Balkans, discussions were carried out in the United Nations regarding the struggle to negotiate between sovereignty of nations and humanitarian intervention. This process evolved in the 2000s into what was termed the 'responsibility to protect' (R2P), the gist of which is that while the responsibility to protect falls on respective states to protect their people, when the state is deemed incapable or unwilling to do this, the responsibility shifts to the international community. See the *Outcome Document of the 2005 United Nations World Summit (A/RES/60/1/ para. 138-140)* at <http://www.un.org/en/ga/search/view_doc.asp?symbol=A/ RES/ 60/1, and *Secretary-General's 2009 Report (A/63/677) on Implementing the Responsibility to Protect*, accessed February 24, 2016, http://www.un.org/en/ga/ search/view_doc.asp?symbol=A/63 /677>. Accessed 24 February 2016.

17. Anne Orford, 'Rethinking the Significance of the Responsibility to Protect Concept', in *Proceedings of the Annual Meeting (American Society of International Law)*, volume 106 (28 March 2012), 30.

decides what protection entails, how to ensure it, and who the rightful authorities are to carry it out.[18] She observes that, for instance, in the 2011 decision to attack Libya, 'it was largely NATO—a regional organisation representing the security interests of Western Europe and North America—that effectively exercised the power to make decisions…'[19] She is concerned that claiming the authority to protect usually results in greater authoritarianism. She highlights the irony that benevolent goals have tended to be connected to the increase in authoritarian security states and that too much focus has been on military action and not on the softer forms of international administrative actions.[20] Talal Asad doubts that global authorities are able to separate the use of violence on the grounds of compassion from the fulfilment of more imperialistic goals, pointing out that in a highly stratified global system these motives can hardly be separated and uninfluenced by these structures and modes of decision making.[21]

As we are witnessing, this cycle of violence and destruction of each other and nature is only escalating. These 'responsible' actions, whether during the cold war in Afghanistan, and more recently in Iraq, Libya and Syria, have only resulted in the creation of even more uncontrollable and unpredictable enemies.[22] Furthermore, so called 'moderate rebels' in Iraq and other places were supported in order to effect regime changes that were supposedly going to bring democracy and human rights. However, the results of this effort to control and

---

18. Orford, 'Rethinking the Significance', 30.
19. Orford, 'Rethinking the Significance' 30.
20. Orford, 'Rethinking the Significance' 30–31.
21. Asad, 'Reflections on Violence', 403–4.
22. These efforts included producing textbooks used in Afghanistan and Pakistan, containing a rather distorted and violent interpretation of various Islamic teachings and texts to indoctrinate young children and youths to motivate them to fight against the Soviets. Joe Stephens and David Ottaway describe some of the contents of the texts, the propaganda, and current concerns about the unintended consequences where this indoctrination has turned against the very people who nurtured this ideology. Joe Stephens and David B. Ottaway, 'From U.S., the ABC's of Jihad', in *The Washington Post*, 23 March 2002 at <https://www.washingtonpost.com/archive/politics/2002/03/23/from-us-the-abcs-of-jihad/d079075a-3ed3-4030-9a96-0d48f6355e54/>. Accessed 25 February 2016. See also the article by Roby Crilly, discussing the same issue, '"Infidels are our enemy": Afghan fighters cherish old American schoolbooks', in *Al Jazeera*, 7 December 2014, <http://america. aljazeera.com/articles/2014/12/7/afghan-fighters-americantextbooks. html>. Accessed 26 February 2016.

shape other people and societies to suit the interests of those with the power to impose their will far and wide have been the violent movements termed as 'Islamic extremism', which have become a further pretext for even more military action. American terrorism expert Robert Pape expresses concern that the war on terror could actually be producing more terrorists, observing that even the former American Secretary of Defense, Donald Rumsfeld, who served under George W. Bush, had wondered whether they were producing more terrorists than they were killing.[23] A similar trend is apparent in our relationship with the rest of nature.

Implications for war with nature

This mode of reasoning that considers only complete control to be responsible action has led us down the path of war with nature, reaping a similar kind of unpredictable and virulent response in the form of climate change and the increase in disasters, and a range of other environmental problems. Scientists Will Steffen et al., speaking of what is known as the 'Great Acceleration', which refers to the profound and rapid changes in the relationship between humans and the natural environment (unprecedented in human history) in the second half of the twentieth century, say:

> …the Great Acceleration marks the phenomenal growth of the global socio-economic system, the human part of the Earth System. It is difficult to overestimate the scale and speed of change. In little over two generations … humanity (or until very recently a small fraction of it) has become a planetary-scale geological force.[24]

---

23. Robert Pape discusses the escalation in terrorism since the 'war on terror' began. He points out that terrorism has been mistakenly blamed on Islam, when in almost all instances of terrorism, the struggle has been over occupation or some other issue. Robert Pape, 'Misguided War on Terror', (plenary Speech at the 2015 Parliament of World Religions, Salt Lake City, Utah, October 17, 2016) at <https://drive.google.com/file/d/0B7t7uxbYqQ7pQllVV2VTVW5KZ0U/edit?pref=2&pli=1>. Accessed 2 November 2015.

24. Will Steffen et al., 'The trajectory of the Anthropocene: The Great Acceleration', in *The Anthropocene Review*, 2/1 (2015): 93–94. Also, see the discussion of this issue in 'Great Acceleration', International Geosphere-Biosphere Programme

The causes of climate change and other environmental problems are many, but a significant aspect of our manipulation of nature has been predicated on how human needs were defined and the policies that were designed to meet them. As articulated in the goals of progress and civilisation noted above regarding development theories, control of our surroundings and the increase in material consumption were considered imperative for well-being. A major emphasis was on the need to increase food production on the grounds that human population was increasing, believing that only large scale, centrally planned industrial level agriculture offered a responsible and effective way to feed the hungry.

While the limited use of chemicals in agriculture began as early as the middle of the Nineteenth century, it was at the end of World War II with the major post-war restructuring that the stockpile of chemicals developed for the war effort were turned into the field of agriculture.[25] This was the period of increased use of chemical fertilisers and pesticides under the auspices of the 'green revolution', followed by the 'white revolution', in the dairy industry, implemented all over the world.[26] With many formerly colonised countries gaining independence and the start of the development era, the spread of these experimental technologies were carried out with speed and on a

---

(IGBP), at <http://www.igbp.net/globalchange/greatacceleration.4.1b8ae20512d b692f2a680001630.html>. Accessed 28 February 2016.

25. Mark S Lesney, 'Agricultural and Food Chemicals: These Compounds nurture the foundation of civilization' at <http://pubs.acs.org/supplements/ chemchronicles2/pdf/023.pdf>. Accessed 5 February 2016. This is a description of the use of chemicals in food production, and now, biofuels. See the article by Michael Pollan, 'What's Eating America', in *Smithsonian Magazine*, 1 July 2006 at <http://www.smithsonianmag.com/people-places/whats-eating-america-21229356/#Lxq6uAcugIUKokW7.99>. Accessed 6 February 2016. Pollan says that the government had a large surplus of ammonium nitrate, which is the main ingredient in making explosives, after World War II, and it also is an excellent source of nitrogen for plants. He quotes Vandana Shiva who said 'We're still eating the leftovers of World War II' in Pollan, 'What's Eating America', 1.

26. Vandana Shiva, *Stolen Harvest: The Hijacking of the Global Food Supply* (Delhi: India Research Press, 2000), 105. In general, this book addresses the problems created by not only the green revolution but the blue and white ones. The latter are respectively applying the same processes of artificially increasing the yields in seafood and dairy products, each having disastrous consequences. See also, by Shiva, *The Violence of the Green Revolution: Third World Agriculture, Ecology and Politics* (Penang: Third World Network, 1991).

large scale. Like James Scott, scientist and well known environmental activist Vandana Shiva also speaks extensively of the reductionistic approach to science that sought to control all aspects of nature as if we were not a part of it; as if the purposes and functions of nature did not have to be taken into account.[27] The organic methods of relying on natural processes that fertilise the crops, the actions of humble soil micro biota and the integrated action of beneficial insects and microbes in balance with the undesirable ones, were considered incapable of providing the absolute control over the production process required for 'responsible food production'. Mixed cropping and agroforestry methods based on greater biodiversity and concomitant security were shunned for industrial models of neat rows of monoculture crops, which are susceptible to decimation by pests.[28] Therefore, industrial agricultural efforts have culminated in the creation of genetically modified crops that are pesticide and herbicide resistant to enable the use of powerful chemicals against pests and weeds. When this resulted in dangerous levels of pollution in waterways and soils they came up with certain (e.g., corn and cotton) genetically modified crops armed with the ability to kill pests (these are Bt crops, which have been genetically engineered to contain the genes of a bacteria *bacillus thuringiensis*, which has insecticidal properties).[29] The purpose was to reduce the use of excess chemicals, but studies point out

----

27. She deals with this issue in several books and articles, see for instance, Vandana Shiva, *Staying Alive: Women, Ecology and Development* (London: Zed Books, 1989). In this work she addresses the dismissal of the local indigenous and women's knowledge and function in the environment.

28. James Scott, *Seeing*, 269, for instance. Several chapters in this book provide a very useful analysis of these processes. The presence of a broader range of plants to attract a variety of beneficial insects and soil microbes creates a balance between beneficial and harmful insects and microbes. Also, when a field is invaded by a particular pest that attacks specific plants, even if these are destroyed, there are other crops that survive. In general, mixing crops tends to confuse pests who may not locate all of their favoured crops in a mixed field. Furthermore, different crops have different mineral and water needs thus the soil in the whole field is not uniformly depleted of the same nutrients. Farmers are able to practice crop rotation and alternate planting to restore the fertility of the soil, making impossible the infestation by a particular pest capable of decimating whole fields of a monoculture broad-acre crop.

29. GC Rotolo et al. analyse the results of their evaluation of genetically modified crops, raising some concerns: GC Rotolo et al., 'Time to re-think the GMO revolution in agriculture', in *Ecological Informatics* 26 (2015).

that the focus of institutions and scientists who are proponents of this practice has been on short-term effects, claiming higher crop yields and less use of chemicals, while attention to longer term and broader effects indicate an increase in the use of chemicals along with other side effects.[30] This has resulted in the threat to our food supply itself with the demise of bees (the main pollinators), the eruption of super weeds, and the accumulation of agricultural residue poisoning waterways.[31] James Scott highlights the fact that the residues were absorbed by organisms along the food chain, including human beings.[32] Rob

---

30. Jeffrey M Smith, *Seeds of Deception: Exposing Corporate and Government Lies About the Safety of Genetically Engineered Food* (Devon: Green Books, 2004). Also, Vandana Shiva *et al*, 'The GMO Emperor Has No Clothes: A Global Citizens Report on the State of GMOs-False Promises, Failed Technologies', publication coordinated by Navdanya International, the International Commission on the Future of Food and Agriculture, and The Centre for Food Safety (CFS), production and printing by SICREA srl, Florence, 18 October 2011 at <www.navdanya.org> or <www.navdanyainternational.it>. Accessed 10 March 2013. This report includes materials, scientific research and citizens' experiences from six continents, launched by Dr Vandana Shiva.

31. Reuters, 'Study: U.S. farmers using more pesticides on "superweeds"'. *NBC News* 2 October 2012 at <http://usnews.nbcnews.com/_news/2012/10/02/14178036-study-us-farmers-using-more-pesticides-onsuperweeds?lite#__utma=238145375.1933819691.1342403074.1349261013.1349317630.170&__utmb=238145375.1.10.1349317630&__utmc=238145375&__utmx=-&__utmz=238145375.1349063535.162.5.utmcsr=google|utmccn=(organic)|utmcmd=organic|utmctr=msn%20news%20usa%20homepage&__utmv=238145375.|8=Earned%20By=msnbc%7Cus%20news=1^12=Landing%20Content=Mixed=1^13=Landing%20Hostname=www.msnbc.msn.com=1^30=Visit%20Type%20to%20Content=Earned%20to%20Mixed=1&__utmk=257183176>. Accessed 4 October 2012. See also Charles M Benbrook, 'Impacts of genetically engineered crops on pesticide use in the U.S. – the first sixteen years', in *Environmental Sciences Europe* 2012, 24:24 at <DOI: 10.1186/2190-4715-24-24>. Accessed 5 February 2016. Benbrook reports that while the use of genetically modified crops was claimed to reduce pesticide and herbicide use, in fact, their use has increased. Furthermore, he points out that this has resulted in new species of herbicide resistant weeds, requiring even more expense to counter them. He also raises the concern regarding public health. James Scott also observes this in *Seeing*, 292. See also, United Nations Environment Programme (UNEP), 'Global Honey Bee Colony Disorders and Other Threats to Insect Pollinators', *United Nations Environment Programme, Emerging Issues*, 2010 at <http://www.unep.org/dewa/Portals/67/pdf/Global_Bee_Colony_Disorder_and_Threats_insect_pollinators.pdf>. Accessed 5 May 2012.

32. Scott, *Seeing*, 291–2.

Nixon points out that Rachel Carson '…famously insisted, herbicides and insecticides should be unmasked as biocides: those supposedly precise weapons in the "war" on pests targeted nothing more precise than life itself'.[33] In the area of dairy and meat, free range and natural organic methods were replaced by the more 'responsible' regime of antibiotics, hormones and factory farming. As environmentalist Vandana Shiva points out, this has resulted in numerous problems for humans and animals alike, from concerns about breast cancer to mad cow disease.[34]

One shocking consequence of globalisation's agro-policies has been the suicides of farmers in different parts of the world. In India alone, nearly thirty thousand farmers committed suicide over a decade.[35] The same has been true in countries like Sri Lanka and Australia.[36] These are mostly because of the debt incurred in having to keep buying the sterile genetically modified seeds and the chemicals required to maintain them, as well as drought due to climate change and a range of other factors, including the policies of the centrally managed agro industry.[37] Furthermore, the Center for Public

---

33. Nixon, *Slow Violence*, xi.
34. Vandana Shiva, *Stolen Harvest*, 37–75. On the effect on chickens, see Tom Philpott, 'Bird Flu is Slamming Factory Farms but Sparing Backyard Flocks. Why?', *Mother Jones*, 20 May, 2015 at <http://www.motherjones.com/tom-philpott/2015/05/ongoing-bird-flu-crisis-stumps-experts>. Accessed 21 September 2015.
35. Vandana Shiva, *Earth Democracy: Justice, Sustainability, and Peace* (Cambridge: South End Press, 2005), 120–21.
36. Sumika Perera, 'Water Privatization and People's Struggle to Protect Common Water Rights in Sri Lanka', presentation at the World Water Forum in Kyoto Japan, March 2003, at <https://www.nadir.org/nadir/initiativ/agp/free/imf/asia/0312waterprivatization.htm>. Accessed 16 September 2007. In Australia, farmer suicides had reached the high numbers of one farmer killing himself every four days. Nick Bryant, 'Australia Drought Sparks Suicides' *BBC News*, 19 October 2006 at <http://news.bbc.co.uk/2/hi/asia-pacific/6065220.stm>. Accessed 15 July 2016. Unlike the situation in Sri Lanka and India, in this case the suicides are not directly related to globalisation and development. Nevertheless, it reveals the rural deprivation created by the dominant model even in a relatively affluent country like Australia, not to mention the drought itself being caused in no small part by the environmentally destructive practices promoted by the dominant structures.
37. The seed's DNA had been manipulated (with the permission of the USDA which gets a percentage from the proceeds of the sale of these seeds) not to reproduce, therefore, they cannot be saved and replanted the next season, forcing farmers to keep buying new batches from the corporations. Shiva, *Stolen Harvest*, 82–3.

Integrity in the United States and several local doctors and scientists in places like Latin America and Asia have raised concerns regarding the epidemic of kidney disease among farmers using industrial chemicals in their farming, resulting in thousands of deaths.[38] A most dramatic effect in the animal kingdom relating to agriculture has been the death of bees (again the causes are a complex range of factors including industrial agricultural and other practices), without whose humble pollinating activities no amount of centralised control could produce most of the crops we eat.[39] In the United States for instance, hives are transported across the country in truckloads in time to pollinate crops due to colony collapse disorder in some of those areas.[40] We see a very different relationship with bees and others within world views and lifestyles based on risk and vulnerability in recognition of our interrelatedness.

---

38. Sasha Chavkin, 'As kidney disease kills thousands across continents, scientists scramble for answers', Center for Public Integrity, 17 September 2012 at <http://www.publicintegrity.org/print/10855>. Accessed 17 October 2012. The Center for Public Integrity points out that while this epidemic is taking place in several places in Latin America, Sri Lanka, and India, although local researchers are observing the connections between the illnesses in these different parts of the world, the wealthy nations and global authorities like the World Health Organization (WHO) fail to do so. Meanwhile, farmers and monks in Sri Lanka for instance, have protested the Food and Agriculture Organization (FAO) asking for compensation for the thousands who have fallen ill, needing kidney transplants, or have died, due to what they allege to be the FAO introduced agro-chemicals. See, Hansani Bandara, 'FAO blamed for chronic kidney disease: Protesting farmers demand compensation for chemical fertiliser victims', in *Sunday Times*, Sri Lanka, 21 October 2012 at <http://www.sundaytimes.lk/121021/news/fao-blamed-for-spread-of-chronic-kidney-disease-17441.html>. Accessed 2 December 2012.

39. UNEP, 'Global Honey Bee Colony'. David Jolly, 'Pesticides Linked to Honeybee Deaths Pose More Risks, European Group Says', *New York Times*, 8 April 2015 at <http://www.nytimes.com/2015/04/09/business/energy-environment/pesticides-probably-more-harmful-than-previously-thought-scientist-group-warns.html?_r=0>. Accessed 21 September 2015.

40. However, several of these trucks have crashed with the millions of honey bees causing chaos on highways. Evan Bush, 'Un-bee-lievable: Truck spills 450 hives along I-5', *Seattle Times*, 17 April 2015 at <http://www.seattletimes.com/seattle-news/millions-of-honeybees-spill-along-i-5-everybodys-been-stung/>. Accessed 21 September 2015.

Embracing risk and vulnerability in recognition of interrelatedness

In the world view discussed above, other creatures do not have the right to live with dignity, and in the case of some, the right even to exist. Recognising ourselves as part of these various cycles and interactions of lives would require planning our livelihoods by engaging in practices that make use of this interplay of lives in the process of producing food and other activities, rather than exerting absolute control in total ignorance of the fact that by violating our rightful place within these webs of life, we have undermined our own wellbeing.

General premises and interrelationship between humans

Judith Butler argues that the experience of injury and loss offers the opportunity for the powerful, for those who have always enjoyed First World privilege, to begin to recognise interdependency, 'that there are others out there on whom my life depends… This fundamental dependency on anonymous others is not a condition that I can will away. No security measure will foreclose this dependency; no violent act of sovereignty will rid the world of this fact'.[41] Thus she points out that final control is not an ultimate value. This is why the ethic of risk advocated by Sharon Welch is promising.

> The ethic of risk is characterised by three elements, each of which is essential to maintain resistance in the face of overwhelming odds: a redefinition of responsible action, grounding in community, and strategic risk-taking. Responsible action does not mean the certain achievement of desired ends but the creation of a matrix in which further actions are possible, the creation of the conditions of possibility for desired changes.[42]

We can help create the conditions necessary for peace and justice, realising that the choices of others can only be influenced and responded to, never controlled.[43]

---

41. Judith Butler, *Precarious Life: The Powers of Mourning and Violence* (New York: Verso, 2004), xii.
42. Welch, *A Feminist Ethic of Risk*, 20.
43. Welch, *A Feminist Ethic of Risk*, 22.

James Scott's approach to addressing social issues emphasises *metis*, the Greek notion of practical knowledge, that which can only come from extended practical experience, having had to adapt to changing circumstances and situations over time.[44] This also includes mutuality, which as he says is more responsive to coordinating 'the diversity of human actions and ...millions of transactions'.[45] Thus he recommends something like Common Law approaches which entail 'not a final codification of legal rules, but rather a set of procedures for continually adapting some broad principles to novel circumstances'.[46] This is because, he says, as Aristotle recognised, many practical decisions cannot be simply subjected to universal rules.[47]

Critical economist Stephen Marglin observes that the Western notion of freedom emphasises individual autonomy; any constraint on this kind of autonomy is perceived as oppression. Other cultures' alternative notions of freedom are not acknowledged.[48] For instance, he points out that Gandhians prioritise control over the self rather than over the environment and others (unlike the development theories) as a prerequisite for freedom. Gandhi says: 'Control over the mind is alone necessary and, when that is attained, man is free like the king of the forest, and his very glance withers the enemy'.[49] It is an approach to freedom and security that perceives one's well-being as inseparable from that of others, human or other. AT Ariyaratne says: 'The lack of spiritual balance is resulting in widespread ecological and environmental problems which also affect the thinking and conduct of human beings'.[50] From the *Sarvodaya* perspective, spiritual mal-

---

44. Scott, *Seeing*, 6, 177–8.
45. Scott, *Seeing*, 344–5.
46. Scott, *Seeing*, 357.
47. Scott, *Seeing*, 322.
48. Stephen A Marglin, 'Towards the Decolonization of the Mind', in *Dominating Knowledge: Development, Culture, and Resistance*, edited by Frederique Apffel Marglin and Stephen A. Marglin (Oxford: Oxford University Press, 1990), 1–3.
49. Mohandas K Gandhi *Hind Swaraj: And Other Writings*, edited by. Anthony J Parel (Cambridge: Cambridge University Press, 1997), 94.
50. AT Ariyaratne is the founder of the Gandhi-Buddhist movement *Sarvodaya Shramadana*, which means the awakening of all through shared labour. It incorporates an alternative form of development and upliftment, but is more holistic than that. George D Bond, *Buddhism at Work: Community Development, Social Empowerment and the Sarvodaya Movement* (Bloomfield, Connecticut: Kumarian Press, 2004), 91.

aise, ecological devastation, mental disturbance, and conflict between humans, are all connected in complex sets of feedback loops. As Ariyaratne elaborates, 'The individual should have a clear and integrated idea as to why, from what and how one has to liberate oneself, one's village community, one's nation and one's world. Unless one's ideological conditioning is non-fragmentary and embraces harmoniously one's own welfare with the welfare of others, one cannot go very far as an agent bringing about effective social change.'[51] Therefore, freedom and emancipation cannot be understood or achieved in competition with and opposition to others, but only in mutual cooperation with them, human or otherwise.

Judith Butler argues that this means that if we as nations and an international community are committed to equality and non-violent cooperation, it is important that we analyse the social and political structures and conditions that give rise to conflicts, in order to change them. She says this means: 'in part, hearing beyond what we are able to hear. And it means as well being open to narration that decenters us from our supremacy....'[52] Hearing beyond what we are able to hear requires a certain degree of epistemic humility, acknowledging that our knowledge structures and technologies may not be able to provide complete knowledge, decentering us from any sense of supremacy. Only by acknowledging others, even non-humans, as partners in our effort to ascertain the circumstances relevant to any situation, and engaging them in our decision process can we arrive at solutions that are mutually beneficial and non-violent. Short of that, as observed by Simone Weil, the strong would tend to impose their will on the weaker parties by force, with the resulting sequence of wars we are witnessing today. Instead of acknowledging vulnerability just like everybody else, as Butler suggests, powerful countries have tended to use war and all forms of violence to make others vulnerable while assuring an illusory invulnerability for themselves.[53] Sallie B King points out that Buddhist ethics and practice depend on the fact

51. AT Ariyaratne, *Buddhism and Sarvodaya: Sri Lankan Experience* (Delhi: Sri Satguru Publications, 1996), 4.

52. Judith Butler, *Precarious Life*, 17–18.

53. Interview by Sabine Hark and Paula-Irene Villa, '"Confessing a passionate state" interview with Judith Butler', in *Feministische Studien*, 2 November 2011, at <http://www.feministische-studien.de/fileadmin/download/pdf/Fem_Stud_text_11_02.pdf>. Accessed 1 March 2016.

that by engaging in good practices such as taking others more and more into account, one gradually becomes less self-centered and even loses this motivation.[54] As she points out, this entails non-attachment to the self, allowing one to overcome a purely one-sided perspective that sees the other as completely at fault, not recognising one's role in the conflict. For instance, Talal Asad highlights that in recent military interventions the rhetoric has been about protecting victims from evil, with the enemy being described as evil, not just wrong, unjust or a threat to one's self-interest.[55] The approach we are talking about is contrary to one that demonises the other; instead, one is able to start 'hearing beyond what one is able to hear' to see the suffering of both sides, consistent with the Buddhist ethic of universal compassion and being able to care about the suffering of others regardless of nationality, race or whatever it is that puts us in opposition to each other. King gives examples from the teachings and practices of a range of Buddhist monks and practitioners such as the Dalai Lama, Sulak Sivaraksa, and Thich Nhat Hanh, regarding the practice of loving kindness which leads one to understand the suffering of those who might hurt us.

King gives the example of the Sri Lankan *Sarvodaya Shramadana*'s 'People's Peace Plan' as an example of non judgmental approach to the resolution of conflict between the two ethnic groups.[56] Instead of blaming one or the other, they seek to identify some of the causes of the conflict, especially poverty, and violence itself, and how each side has contributed, emphasising the need for spiritual wholeness to overcome some of these structural issues. As an alternative development movement, they highlight even more the significance of their efforts to awaken all through creating nonviolent ways of life and social structures, considering this to be integral to the construction

---

54. Sallie B King, *Socially Engaged Buddhism* (Honolulu: University of Hawaii Press, 2009), 31. King is a religious scholar.
55. Asad, 'Reflections on Violence', 423–4. Asad discusses the use of Reinhold Niebuhr's understanding of combating evil in which evil evokes a notion of something that is a greater threat beyond just human errors and misbehaviour, in the combatting of which one may be justified in overstepping ordinary notions of right and wrong. As Asad points out, more and more humanitarians are using this term in regard to those they oppose.
56. King, *Socially Engaged Buddhism*, 37–8.

of genuine peace, because of the interdependence of everything.[57] They also have a branch called the *Shanthi Sena* (peace brigade) to which many of the youth in *Sarvodaya* villages belong. They participate in a range of activities including first aid and engaging in programs of exchanges between various ethnic communities to create love and understanding. This involves having people in one ethnic group, especially youth in the *Shanthi Sena*, staying with families of another ethnic group and engaging in shared labour on various village projects. These have been evaluated positively by many.[58] Instead of relying on violence or increasing legislation to control the other's behaviour, they engage in the risky behaviour of treating the others as equal partners in creating not just some *modus vivendi* but more like a beloved community (Martin Luther King's term) or a mutually awakened (*Sarvodaya*) society. In this situation, the outcome is dependent on the interplay of one's own actions and responses as well as that of the other, as Welch's quote above indicates, it creates a matrix of possibilities through mutual influencing of others.

Developing goodwill and friendships will more likely maintain peaceful and cooperative responses in the long run, unlike laws or bombing aimed at holding the other at bay. The people who participate in the *Shanthi Sena* program say that they start off as strangers with the families of other ethnic groups and leave as family; in fact, during the few days they spend with these families, they refer to each other using familial terms.[59] The executive director of the program observes that we will never see any of the participants lift a weapon against the other ethnic groups at any time in the future because of the love and understanding they have developed through these programs.[60] Not the assurance obtained by bombs but through the sharing of vulnerability, risk, and loving compassion.

---

57. George D Bond, 'Sarvodaya's Pursuit of Peace', in *Buddhism, Conflict and Violence in Modern Sri Lanka*, edited by Mahinda Deegalle (London: Routledge, 2006), 231.

58. Bond, *Buddhism at Work*, 36.

59. Observed at Shanthi Sena camp, 20–21 August 2009, Puttalam, Sri Lanka.

60. Statement by Ravindra Kandage in a short documentary film with clips from a Shanthi Sena camp filmed in 2007. This was during the war, which only ended in 2009. See 'Shanthi Sena Film with English Subtitle'. VOB, *Shanthi Sena*, 29 June 2012, at <https://www.youtube.com/watch?v=6dTbqX5yQ1M>. Accessed 7 November 2013.

Another large scale activity that Sarvodaya engages in is organising mass loving-kindness (*metta*) meditations with thousands of people participating, even during the war. The idea is to engage in this spiritual practice together to cultivate loving kindness at a national level, to replace hostility with harmony. King points out that about 10 percent of the country's population had participated in this.[61] Observing that some may wonder how effective these efforts are, she cites recent neuro scientific studies demonstrating that these practices stimulate the parts of the brain responsible for empathy and maternal love (this increases when the meditator has more experience in compassion meditation), and lower activity in the parts associated with differentiation between the self and other.[62] According to AT Ariyaratne, this was part of the effort to change the 'psychosphere'.[63] Buddhist scholar and eco-philosopher Joanna Macy describes how these meditation activities are carried out along with village-to-village link up programs between Sinhalese and Tamil villages, where they engage in food sharing and volunteering to rebuild homes. She gives the example of how a Sinhalese village had filled two lorries (trucks) with roofing material as soon as they heard of the opportunity to go and help Tamil villagers in the north. So it is in this sort of context that masses of people are brought together for meditation sessions. Macy, who participated in one of the biggest such events with 650,000 people, observes:

> they made the biggest silence I ever heard. After prayers from Buddhist, Hindu and Muslim clerics, and in the intervals between Dr Ariyaratne's words, guiding us in mindfulness of breath, in loving kindness and firm resolve for peace, the silence deepened. I thought: this is the sound of bombs and land mines not exploding, of rockets not launched and machine guns laid aside. It is possible, for us all.[64]

---

61. King, *Socially Engaged Buddhism*, 50.
62. King, *Socially Engaged Buddhism*, 51, 86. She mentions the largest such meditation held in 2002 with 650,000 gathered in Anuradhapura. Joanna Macy was present at this one and describes it.
63. Joanna Macy, 'Sarvodaya Means "Everybody Wakes Up"' *EarthLight Magazine*, 45, 2002 at <http://www.earthlight.org/essay45_macy_pff.html>. Accessed 9 March 2016.
64. Macy, 'Sarvodaya Means'.

George Bond points out that through this critical mass of spiritual consciousness, Sarvodaya seeks to transfer power to the people as a challenge to the powers and structures that have created the violence. They emphasise that peace has to come through such grass roots efforts, making armies and the politicians unnecessary.[65] And as Sarvodaya argues, 'the war cannot be won; it can only be transcended'. That is, as I have argued so far, the final control sought by the dominant powers is not possible. The alternative methods of risk entailing the creation of matrixes of mutual actions offer the opportunity to actually transcend the causes and conditions of the conflict, war and violence.

Interrelationship with the rest of nature

This approach is no different when dealing with non-human species. In a Hindu-Buddhist world view animals are also interconnected with humans on the cosmic path to enlightenment and nirvana. AT Ariyaratne and Nandasena Ratnapala point out that the well-being of animals is an essential component of any notion of justice or democracy.[66] Noting the respect given to animals in Buddhism, Christopher Key Chapple asserts that the understanding of all humans and animals as undergirded by the ultimate reality Brahman, affirms their interrelatedness, such that one cannot harm another without at the same time harming oneself.[67] According to Ariyaratne, the error of modern Western civilisation is that it is trying to master nature as

---

65. Bond, 'Sarvodaya's Pursuit of Peace', 228, 230.

66. Ariyaratne, *Buddhism and Sarvodaya*, 67. Nandasena Ratnapala, *Buddhist Democratic Political Theory and Practice* (Ratmalana, Sri Lanka: Sarvodaya Vishva Lekha Publications, 1997), vi, xi–xiii. There is historic precedence with the Fourth century emperor Asoka establishing healthcare for animals, see *The Edicts of Asoka*, edited and translated by NA Nikam and Richard McKeon (Chicago: University of Chicago Press, 1959), 64–5.

67. Christopher Key Chapple, *Non-Violence to Animals, Earth, and Self in Asian Traditions* (Delhi: Sri Satguru Publications, 1995), 23–4. There is increasing evidence in agriculture and in human health to indicate that killing micro-organisms and species we consider to be pests is negatively impacting our livelihood, food production and health (for instance the recent findings on allergies caused by insufficient exposure to micro-organisms). See for instance, Graham A Rook, 'Regulation of the immune system by biodiversity from the natural environment: An ecosystem service essential to health', *PNAS*

if humans are not an integral part of it.[68] He says that the story of development is based on the kind of science that separates the scientist from the discoveries, from others, from themselves, and the processes that are the outcome of his/her work, and has led to greed and exploitation of fellow humans and non-humans.

Consistent with these Buddhist perspectives, trans-species psychologists Gay Bradshaw and Mary Watkins argue: 'Much as liberation psychologists are asked to help change conditions that dehumanise, trans-species' psychologists are called to address conditions that de-nature humans by separating them through false species' distinctions'.[69] This distinction, based on a notion that animals lack a psyche, informed the Western human collective identity and ego construct, functioning as a primary cultural organising principle. However, increasing scientific evidence has led to the acceptance in science and society that the brain and psyche are trans-species.[70] This of course has important implications for our understanding of our relationship with other species. They say 'a multi-species science and ethos includes other species as partners in decision-making, culture-making, and community meaning-making', which leads to a de-privileging of human language.[71] This is consistent with the Bud-

---

(*Proceedings of the National Academy of Sciences*), November 12, 2013, 110/46 at <doi.10.1073/pnas.1313731110>. Accessed 17 September 2015.

68. Ariyaratne, *Buddhism and Sarvodaya*, 56.

69. GA Bradshaw and Mary Watkins, 'Trans-Species Psychology: Theory and Praxis', The Kerulos Center at <http://www.kerulos.org/wp-content/uploads/2014/07/Bradshaw-WatkinsSpringFinalized.pdf> 4. Accessed 27 May 2013. They point out that even those such as Paolo Friere who wrote on the pedagogy of the oppressed, explicitly differentiated humans from animals, excluding the latter from the sphere of concern. Ignatio Martin-Baro who wrote on the need for psychologists to contribute to conditions that humanise did not include animals or humans' relationships to them.

70. Bradshaw and Watkins, 'Trans-Species Psychology', 7.

71. Bradshaw and Watkins, 'Trans-Species Psychology', 14. There are many scientists and other scholars demonstrating the continuity with other species and the interrelated nature of knowledge and morality. Frans de Waal, *Good Natured: The Origins of the Right and Wrong in Humans and Other Animals* (Cambridge: Harvard University Press, 1996), 50–2. Jane Good all was among the first to dispel the belief in one of the primary characteristics of humans as toolmakers as forming the basis of our separation from other animals who were considered to be incapable of this, when she observed chimpanzees using tools. Frans de Waal, *Chimpanzee Politics: Power and Sex Among Apes* (Baltimore: Johns Hopkins

dhist emphasis on the inseparability of humans and other species in notions of democracy and wellbeing.

Among those who abide by their Buddhist beliefs and values in Sri Lanka, the use of pesticides and herbicides are eschewed because they are inconsistent with *ahimsa* (non-harm). Instead, they practice the sort of agro-ecoforestry and mixed cropping mentioned above, relying on the balance created by the interplay between beneficial and harmful insects, recognising that even these latter have a right to live. A system in which food crops are mixed in with forest trees and tanks, not the neat rows of mono crops deemed efficient and controllable by the modernists. The life and activity of all these species are dependent on and imperative to human life and actions. These are effective micro systems that act as water conservation systems which are also high in biodiversity, thereby providing resilience in the face of inclement weather conditions, and disease or pests.[72]

University Press, 1989), 18. Japanese scientists have also noted the capacity for culture and the ability to pass it on to future generations in their observations of the Japanese macaques. De Waal, among others, has contributed a lot regarding some semblance of society, peace making, and political manipulations, among chimpanzees. Frans de Waal, *Peace making Among Primates* (Cambridge: Harvard University Press, 1990). Recently the relationship of religions to animals and the implication of these beliefs for the environment, law, and social justice has been addressed by several scholars. See for instance, *A Communion of Subjects: Animals in Religion, Science, and Ethics* edited by Paul Waldau and Kimberly Patton, (New York: Columbia University Press, 2006). Frans BM de Waal, 'Primates: A Natural Heritage of Conflict Resolution', in *Science, New Series,* 289/5479 (28 July 2000). See also, Nicolas Lescureux, 'Towards the necessity of a new interactive approach integrating ethnology, ecology and ethology in the study of the relationship between Kyrgyz stockbreeders and wolves', *Social Science Information,* 45/3 (2006): 463–78.

72. Lakshman Yapa, 'The Poverty Discourse and the Poor in Sri Lanka', *Transactions of the Institute of British Geographers, New Series,* 23/1 (1998), 102. About the water conservation ecosystem see, DLO Mendis, *Alternative Development: An Anthology: Volume 1, Part II, Remember Your Humanity: If you want peace, prepare for peace* (Ratmalana: Vishva Lekha, 2005), 61; Sara J. Scherr and Jeffrey A. McNeely (editors) *Farming with Nature: The Science and Practice of Ecoagriculture* (Washington: Island Press, 2007), 233, 241. The following discuss the importance of this kind of agro-forest-ecosystems in general: Gotz Schroth et al., (editors), *Agroforestry and Biodiversity Conservation in Tropical Landscapes* (Washington: Island Press, 2004), 8, 22, 28, 29, 66, 70, 153–97. Anoja Wickramasinghe, 'Anthropogenic Factors and Forest Management in Sri Lanka', *Applied Geography,* 17/2 (1997), at <doi:10.1016/S0143-6228(97)00003-9>.

These systems do not also neatly separate the food growing, nature conservation and religious activity, making it hard for the colonial powers and modernist reformers to appreciate the scientific values of this seeming chaos until recently.[73] Unlike the conventionally trained zoologists' recommendations to deal with crop raiding elephants (a result of modernised agriculture and development) by creating neatly demarcated electric fences, keeping animals and humans separate, the indigenous system is based on a symbiotic relationship.[74] Instead

---

Anoja Wickramasinghe, *Deforestation, Women and Forestry: The Case of Sri Lanka*, (Utrecht: International Books, 1994).

73. What seemed to be undue reverence and anthropomorphic characteristics ascribed to flora and fauna have increasingly been validated by scientists. For a discussion of the significance of indigenous agricultural methods, see for instance, Gordon Prain et al. (editors), *Biological and Cultural Diversity: The Role of Indigenous Agricultural Experimentation in Development* (London: Intermediate Technology Publications, 1999). Many of the agricultural and other activities within the ecosystem involve religious rituals, dances and songs, deemed irrelevant to the actual activities on hand by most modernists, but they are embodied forms of epistemologies. Bill Mollison, *Permaculture: A Designer's Manual* (Sisters Creek, Tasmania: Tagari Publications, 1988), 2, 97; David Holmgren, *Permaculture: Principles & Pathways Beyond Sustainability* (Hepburn, Victoria: Holmgren Design Services, 2002), xvii; John Porter *et al.* (editors), 'The Value of Producing Food, Energy, and Ecosystem Services within an Agro-Ecosystem', in *Ambio*, 38/4 (2009); Anoja Wickramasinghe, 'Adam's Peak Sacred Mountain Forest', *The Importance of Sacred Natural Sites for Biodiversity Conservation* (Proceedings of the International Workshop held in Kunming and Xishuangbanna Biosphere Reserve, People's Republic of China, 17–20 February 2003), United Nations Educational, Scientific and Cultural Organization, UNESCO, at <http://unesdoc.unesco.org/images/0013/001333/133358e.pdf>. Accessed 2 November 2012.

74. See separate opinion of Vice President of the International Court of Justice on the decision based on the 1997 case concerning Gabcikovo-Nagymaros (Hungary/ Slovakia) Project. Christopher G. Weeramantry, *Environmental Aspects of Sri Lanka's Ancient Irrigation System* (Ratmalana, Sri Lanka: Sarvodaya Vishva Lekha Publishers, 2000). He discusses (page 18) the system of combining human and ecological interests and the Buddhist mandate that the land belongs to the animals as well. The following describe the symbiotic system where humans and animals rely on each other, especially the elephants, showing that cooperation without absolute control provided greater security than the modern system which has given rise to so much conflict: Mangala De Silva and Padma Kumari De Silva, *The Sri Lankan Elephant: Its Evolution, Ecology and Conservation* (Colombo: WHT Publications, 2007). HIE. Katugaha et al., 'A long-term study on the dynamics of the elephant (*Elephas Maximus*) population in Ruhunu National Park, Sri Lanka', *Biological Conservation* 89 (1999), 58.

of shooting at raiding elephants, the practicing Buddhists engage in prayers, chants and pleading with the animals; an approach they find effective. Sarvodaya members point out that none of them would ever use violence against an elephant, and in return no elephant had killed one of them.[75] This is a sense of security that comes, not from the power of the gun but spiritual practice, loving kindness, and co operation from all species. Another practice among Buddhist villagers harvesting honey is to approach the hive after meditation, thus keeping themselves and the bees calm without using smoke or protective gear.[76] Harvesting honey in the forest includes chants asking the Gods for protection and forgiveness from the bees.[77] Some alternative natural beekeepers in the West, influenced by the teachings of the founder of biodynamic farming, Rudolf Steiner, embrace a similar approach of sharing vulnerability with the bees by not wearing any protective gear.[78] This is clearly 'risky' from a control ethic perspective, but one that relies on mutual trust without the assurance of protective gear and smoke providing control over the bees' actions.

---

75. Interviews (5, 31 August 2009 and 1–3 September 2009) among Sarvodaya members and others in the Tanamalwila, Kitulkote areas in Sri Lanka. On elephants recognising ethnic groups or specific groups of people, see, Lucy A Bates *et al.*, 'Elephants Classify Human Ethnic Groups by Odor and Garment Color', *Current Biology*, 17 (20 November 2007).

76. Interview, 5 August 2009, Thanamalwila, Sri Lanka.

77. JB Disanayaka, *The Monk and the Peasant* (Colombo: State Printing Corporation, 1993), 117. Part of the reason for the chanting is the acknowledgement that at some level the bees are being violated.

78. Green, Kelsey and Franklin Ginn, 'The Smell of Selfless Love: Sharing Vulnerability with Bees in Alternative Apiculture', *Environmental Humanities*, Volume 4 (2014): 149–70. The authors analyse this approach as an ethical mode along the lines of Judith Butler's arguments discussed above. The beekeepers embody a moral and spiritual framework very much like the Buddhist villagers', in recognition of interrelatedness. The commitment to not wearing protective gear has to do with the concomitant attitude that comes with whether one approaches bees with the gear or in a spirit of love, respect and shared vulnerability. As in the case of the Buddhist villagers as well, the approach taken by the beekeepers influences the behaviour of the bees, who also remain calm at the approach of humans who seem friendly, 163.

Conclusion

It is clear that the ethic of control is the inevitable approach that ensues from the non-recognition of interrelatedness, because as the examples above illustrate, when we don't perceive our interrelatedness, and that our fate is inextricably interrelated to the others', we seek to solve problems by controlling the other, reaping devastating consequences. However, an ethic of risk and vulnerability flows naturally out of a deep recognition of interrelatedness. That is, such recognition, as in the examples above, automatically leads to ways of relating and living that embrace vulnerability in a spirit of cooperation. The most significant point is that the approach taken, with concomitant lifestyle, determines the response elicited from the other.[79] An ethic of interrelatedness and risk provides a more viable approach to the many 'wicked problems' identified by Valerie Brown et al., facing the world today.[80] They argue for a new approach that is more open-ended, using more imagination and multiple inputs and feedback (multiple matrices of possibility), unlike conventional approaches. Otherwise, we are doomed to continue the current path of war with nature and each other.[81]

---

79. It is important to note that the recognition of interrelatedness and the ethic of risk that arises out of it are not just about individual decisions and actions, but embodies a whole lifestyle and way of relating to human and others, as is apparent in the examples above. By living in symbiotic systems with elephants, bees or other humans, some of the problems that arise in our current societies do not even occur, and those that do, are dealt with in ways that do not seek absolute control and do not elicit violent and vengeful responses.

80. Valerie A Brown, John A Harris and Jacqueline Y Russell, *Tackling Wicked Problems: Through the Trans disciplinary Imagination* (New York: Earth scan, 2010). Wicked problems as the authors understand them are ones that defy simple solutions based on existing modes of functioning.

81. Brown, Harris and Russell, *Tackling Wicked Problems*, 6, and especially the introductory chapter 'Towards a Just and Sustainable Future'. Climate change is one of the major issues they identify.

Oil beyond War and Peace: Rethinking the Meaning of Matter

Deborah Guess

War and ecological impact

Living in the time of the Anthropocene[1] it seems axiomatic that the natural world, like the human beings who wield such influence over it, will often be damaged through the human act of warfare.[2] Such damage has occurred since ancient times, sometimes intentionally in the form of tactical 'earth scorching' methods and sometimes unintentionally in what is euphemistically termed 'collateral damage.'[3] One of the most dramatic media images of the effect of war on the environment is of the deliberate release and burning of oil during the First Gulf War. On 16 January 1991 Iraq began firing Kuwaiti wells at Wafra oil field, and three days later began releasing oil from the Sea Island tanks into the Persian Gulf. By 21 February the oil had reached Abu Ali Island on the Saudi Arabian coast. It is not known how much oil was released: estimates range from 0.5 to 12 million barrels, with the most frequently cited estimate being 6 to 8 million barrels. The U.S. General Accounting Offices found that of a total of 904 oil wells,

---

1. The term 'Anthropocene' was popularised by Dutch atmospheric chemist Paul Crutzen who coined the term in 2000 to describe the present geological era as one in which human activity so extensively influences the biophysical world that our species now determines the fate of both other species and natural systems. Paul J Crutzen and Hans Günter Brauch (editors), *Paul J. Crutzen: A Pioneer on Atmospheric Chemistry and Climate Change in the Anthropocene*, Springer Briefs on Pioneers in Science and Practice: Nobel Laureates (Basel: Springer Nature, 2016), 247.
2. Susan D Lanier-Graham, *The Ecology of War: Environmental Impacts of Weaponry and Warfare* (New York: Walker, 1993), 3.
3. For examples see Lanier-Graham, *The Ecology of War*, 3–7.

only 106 remained intact before Iraqi troops began withdrawal on 23 February 1991.[4]

At the time, it was predicted that this highly spectacular event would cause extensive ecological damage. Subsequent scientific reports also suggested environmental disruption. Jurgen Brauer examines the damage caused by the 1991 Gulf War and concludes that there has been little, perhaps no, recovery of plant and animal communities in mudflats and salt-marshes in sheltered bays, and that some of the mangrove stands in the bays just west of Abu Ali Island may be irreversibly damaged. Further, Brauer considers it highly likely that the soil of the Kuwaiti desert (and its dependent flora and fauna) would have been damaged from being churned during the Iraqi invasion, from the putting out of oil fires, and from the subsequent expansion of oil facilities.[5]

A less expected outcome of the 1991 Gulf War, according to Brauer, is that despite the evidence of damage he recounts, the extensive scale of ecological disaster predicted at the time has not eventuated. In part he considers this due to fortuitous local geography: the Gulf is shallow with high levels of evaporation and salinity; air pollution was quickly and widely dispersed by wind, and water pollution dispersed by current.[6] In high-energy sandy beaches and rocky shores, recolonisation began within seven years of the end of the war.[7] In terms of air quality, groundwater contamination, and most aspects of the marine environment, it was hard, some years after the war, to determine significant war-related impact, at least for Kuwait and Saudi Arabia.[8] Although at the time of his writing in 2009 Brauer felt it was too early to assess fully the long-term effects, he felt that overall 'the effect [of the war] was probably substantial but not irreversible.

---

4. This data on the Gulf War is taken from Jurgen Brauer, *War and Nature: The Environmental Consequences of War in a Globalized World* (Lanham: Altamira, 2009), 81–2.

5. Brauer, *War and Nature*, 157.

6. Brauer, *War and Nature*, 85–6, 169.

7. Brauer, *War and Nature*, 109.

8. Brauer notes that: 'Information on damages suffered on Iraqi territory is scant … it should at least be considered that the environmental, let alone human, impact of the war on Iraq was possibly worse than that on Kuwait and Saudi Arabia. … Unlike for Kuwait and Saudi Arabia, the international community did not (or could not) provide post war environmental monitoring and remediation assistance to Iraq.' Brauer, *War and Nature*, 82.

There is nothing in the literature that suggests altogether altered eco-systems.'[9]

Brauer's work brings to light two issues. First, there is a lack of studies on the specifically ecological impact of war. Brauer notes that war studies tend to be carried out from political and humanitarian perspectives, with few studies having been conducted from the perspective of physical habitat, and even fewer on ecosystemic functioning as a whole: Brauer's own research on the Vietnam and Persian Gulf wars is among the few exceptions.[10] The shortage of ecological studies means that 'on the whole environmental measurement in war is fiendishly difficult'.[11] This is not to say that in spite of the release and burning of huge amounts of oil during the war, ecosystems in and around the Gulf are thriving: as discussed above and below, Brauer is clear that they are not. Rather, what he claims is that the available information is insufficient to make a strong call either way regarding the ecological impact of the Gulf (and other) wars.

Second (and especially relevant to the question of war and ecology), it is not always the case that war is necessarily more ecologically detrimental than peace. This counters the intuitive notion that because war is highly damaging to human well-being, this is necessarily the case for the other-than-human parts of the world too. It is indisputable that during times of war the increased production of weaponry and other military supplies will lead to a larger military ecological footprint than occurs in peace-time. But it is also the case that war tends to suppress non-military economic and industrial activity, and this fall in non-military levels of production and consumption can lead to a decreased ecological footprint overall. This argument is supported by John McNeill who, while acknowledging that there can often be extensive damaged caused to the environment by war, also notes the way that war temporarily lessens 'some ordi-

---

9. Brauer, *War and Nature*, 110.
10. Brauer, *War and Nature*, 158, 170. Brauer's work on the Gulf War is possible because that war is unique in having 'elicited a huge amount of scientific interest and political and financial support for damage assessment' (Brauer, *War and Nature*, 82).
11. Brauer, *War and Nature*, xv.

nary environmental pressures' for example in the way that fish stocks in the North Atlantic regenerated during World War II.[12]

Like McNeill, Brauer does not question that war brings ecological destruction, but when he compares this with the ecological damage incurred during times of peace he concurs that war can at times be environmentally beneficial. For example, the Korean War in the early 1950s left a 'demilitarized zone that today is a haven for wildlife seen nowhere else on the peninsula,'[13] and in countries where mine fields restrict human resettlement wildlife refuges have effectively been created.[14] Although the use of herbicides such as Agent Orange in the Vietnam war is often cited as an instance of war-induced ecological destruction, Brauer found that the environment in Vietnam, Cambodia, and Laos, although significantly damaged at the time of the Vietnam war, by 2009 had a stronger ecology than neighbouring countries such as Burma, Indonesia, Malaysia and Thailand which were relatively unaffected by the war.[15]

In the case of the Persian Gulf, Brauer considers that the poor quality of ecosystems is not only, or even primarily, attributable to war-related spills but to peacetime impacts such as regularly occurring pollution from plastics and metals, coastal in filling, and the destruction of mangrove areas and coral reefs on account of commercial development and land reclamation efforts.[16] Brauer notes: 'it is remarkable that a large part, perhaps even the larger part, of these damages are attributable to pre- and post-war peacetime commerce rather than to the war of 1991.'[17] Further, the volume of oil spilled and burnt in the Gulf War is not as significant as might appear at first glance when compared with the 'average annual volume of Gulf oil spills estimated at between 250,000 barrels, equal to the 1989 spill at

---

12. John McNeill, *Something New under the Sun: An Environmental History of the Twentieth-Century World* (New York: Norton, 2000), 346.

13. Brauer, *War and Nature*, xvii.

14. Brauer, *War and Nature*, xvii.

15. Brauer, *War and Nature*, 167. Susan Lanier-Graham's work does not go into the subject as thoroughly as Brauer and usually argues more strongly than Brauer that: 'The environment nearly always suffers during war'. She nevertheless agrees with Brauer that there are sometimes positive impacts of war. Lanier-Graham, *The Ecology of War*, xxvii.

16. Brauer, *War and Nature*, 108.

17. Brauer, *War and Nature*, 108.

Prince William Sound in Alaska, to more than one million barrels of oil per year'.[18] Brauer concludes that 'the thesis that war's effects on nature are unambiguously detrimental turns out to be too simple. Just as war imposes costs on nature, war also bestows benefits'.[19]

This is not to ignore the extensive damage that war can cause to the entire, more-than-human,[20] natural world. Neither is it to deny that as technology becomes more sophisticated the potential for destruction increases: nuclear activity, for instance, is a form of war that especially threatens extreme injury, if not complete anni-hilation, to more-than-human natural systems in their entirety. But it does claim that although war usually intensifies the violence inflicted on the human part of nature, it can at times offer the rest of nature a 'macabre reprieve from human incursion'.[21] This suggests that the terms 'war' and 'peace' essentially refer to human life and well-being: it is uncertain how they might meaningfully be applied to the other-than-human parts of the world. Brauer uses the term 'war' metaphorically to argue that in effect a constant 'war' is being waged by the human species on the natural world during so-called times of peace: 'When the guns are silent, nature does not necessarily recover because by all appearances peace (economic development) is a continuation of war on nature'.[22] Brauer cites Jeffrey McNeely, chief scientist of the International Union for Conservation of Nature and Natural Resources, who argues that: 'While war is bad for biodiver-sity, peace can be worse … market forces are often more destructive than military forces.'[23] Writer and critic James Fallows agrees, saying that: 'peace is a bigger environmental problem than war'.[24]

The notion that peace-time economic activity can inflict as much, sometimes more, damage on natural entities and ecological systems than military activity does not detract from the moral urge to reduce,

---

18. Brauer, *War and Nature*, 82.
19. Brauer, *War and Nature*, xvii.
20. The phrase 'more-than-human' is used to refer to the entire natural order, including human beings. It emphasises the important point that humankind is part of nature and yet at the same time that the biophysical world is far more extensive than just the human parts of it.
21. Brauer, *War and Nature*, 166.
22. Brauer, *War and Nature*, 149.
23. Brauer, *War and Nature*, xvii.
24. Cited by Brauer, *War and Nature*, 167–8.

cease or prevent war. Rather, it invites us to enlarge our understanding of violence and human-inflicted damage beyond the sphere of war and to consider the damage that can be inflicted on the natural order as a consequence of our 'normal' peace-time commercial and industrial activity. This expanded perspective begins a process of rethinking the distinction between the concepts of 'war' and 'peace' and invites an ecological critique of human action not primarily in relation to war but to what has become the standard neo-liberal economic paradigm: 'From an environmental point of view, war preparation and war are just other forms of production and consumption.'[25]

This idea reveals the extent to which our perspectives on war are fostered by anthropocentric assumptions and concerns.[26] Anthropocentric attitudes and behaviour tend to be critiqued in ecological philosophy for two reasons. First, they disregard the interests and value of other-than-human nature and can there by sanction a thoughtless use and abuse of the world which has both caused and exacerbated the present ecological crisis. Second, they diminish human beings by ignoring our common ancestry with the entire biophysical world and there by isolate us from the rest of nature of which we are an integral part and on which our lives depend. The task of critiquing human-centred attitudes is often difficult because anthropocentrism is a powerful, habitual and often unconsciously-held part of the Western world view. It can be very hard to re-focus our intellectual, ethical and imaginative vision beyond the human to encompass sufficiently widely our broader biophysical context. Yet the present and worsening ecological situation seems to call for such a shift of human vision.

---

25. Brauer, *War and Nature*, 4.
26. 'Anthropocentrism' is used here not in its philosophically 'trivial' or tautological sense which claims that anything said or done by a human being is inevitably anthropocentric. Instead the term is used in the stronger sense of describing and critiquing a form of species selfishness or egocentrism especially when it unquestioningly places human interests above the interests of the non-human 'other'. Peter Singer's term 'speciesism' articulates the problematic nature of species-centredness rather effectively because it calls to mind the better known terms 'sexism' and 'racism' which are already accepted and commonly used critical terms. 'Anthropocentrism' is used here as a preferred term to 'speciesism' both because it is a more elegant-sounding word and because it is a more frequently used term in ecophilosophical and ecotheological literature.

Vital Materialism

Ecological philosophy tends to critique and resist anthropocentrism in favour of a position which advocates what philosopher Warwick Fox calls a more 'egalitarian attitude on the part of humans towards all entities in the ecosphere—including humans'.[27] For Australian ecological philosopher Val Plumwood, a move away from anthropocentrism entails questioning the set of hierarchical dualisms (by which she means binary oppositions such as: human-nonhuman, subject-object, culture-nature) in which, she argues, Western Modern thought is immersed and which have underpinned various centric understandings including anthropocentrism.[28] The dualism of humankind-nature, for example, exaggerates differences between the human and the non-human, valorising human beings as subjects and primary actors over against the rest of the natural world which is seen as a set of objects whose sole or primary purpose is to be acted on and manipulated.

One way to discuss the spillage and firing of oil in the Gulf War of 1991 from a perspective which takes into account an ecological ethos is to question, or at least soften, the rigidity implied in the hierarchical dualism of life and matter. An overly sharp segregation between life and matter in the Enlightenment and Modern eras has tended to valorise life (especially human life) as the active agent, and to demote matter as inherently inert, inactive, passive, and incapable of anything resembling agency. From the perspective of a life-matter dualism, material parts of the Persian Gulf such as oil, sea, air and sand are objects without agency or significance except in the way they are acted upon by living beings, and especially by human beings. Like other dualisms, the quarantine between life and matter provides a foundation for an anthropocentric approach.

A questioning of the sharp segregation between the living and the non-living might lead to a changed perspective which recognises the complex interrelationship between the various entangled entities and actions that are involved in an event such as the Gulf War. Instead of the Gulf War being seen only from political, economic, cultural

---

27. Warwick Fox, *Toward a Transpersonal Ecology: Developing New Foundations for Environmentalism* (Boston: Shambhala, 1990), 20.
28. Val Plumwood, *Environmental Culture: The Ecological Crisis of Reason* (London: Routledge, 2002).

and humanitarian perspectives, it might also be seen in relation to the way the climate of the Gulf deals with polluted air or the ability of Persian Gulf biota to reproduce after an oil spill. It might also facilitate a closer look at the machines and technologies that extract, store, spill and burn the contested fossil fuel, the various civilian and military uses to which oil is put, and so on. A re-imagining of the meaning of matter allows oil to be seen in a broader category, not only as an 'object' to be used in human-driven Middle Eastern and global political-economic conflict but also in terms of its own subjectivity and history, for example as the buried remains of millennia of fossilised trees that once grew on Earth. To envision 'life' and 'matter' horizontally rather than dualistically is to treat oil less as an object and more as a subject which has the ability to influence the biota of the Persian Gulf in radically different ways depending on whether it remains in the earth, is released to the air or sea, is set on fire, and so on. A more horizontal view of life and matter implies also a more horizontal view of human kind and nature. An understanding of ourselves as more dynamically inter-related to the non-human parts of nature resonates with a more ecologically focused and critical attitude with respect to our way of living and to our current economic paradigm.

One version of a philosophical-political re-thinking of the nature and meaning of matter which challenges life-matter dualism occurs in the body of work known as vital materialism (also articulated as 'new materialisms'.)[29] New, or vital, materialism contests the idea that matter is essentially inert or passive, positing instead 'the vitality of matter and the lively powers of material formations'.[30] Matter, argues Jane Bennett, is to be seen as 'vibrant' not only because it has a capacity to impede human intentions but because it also has its own agency or force: as an actant matter has the ability, or the potential, to self-organise and in a way which is congregational rather than atomistic.[31] Bennett emphasises that her aim is not to 'overstate the thinginess

---

29. The work of Jane Bennett is used here as the primary example of this body of thought. Jane Bennett, *Vibrant Matter: A Political Ecology of Things* (Durham: Duke University Press, 2010). In addition, I refer to a collection of essays on the topic in Diana Coole and Samantha Frost (editors), *New Materialisms: Ontology, Agency, and Politics* (Durham: Duke University Press, 2010).
30. Bennett, *Vibrant Matter*, vii.
31. Bennett, *Vibrant Matter*, viii, 7, 20.

or fixed stability of materiality', but to 'theorise a materiality that is as much force as entity, as much energy as matter, as much intensity as extension'.[32] Matter is for Bennett 'a vitality' which is at work both inside the human person and outside of us.[33] An example of the vitality of matter given by Bennett is in the way food (dietary fats for instance) can alter human moods, or the way that garbage can generate chemical compounds such as methane.[34]

Bennett's thought avoids a sharp subject-object distinction: she emphasises that an actant (by which she means a source of action, either human or non-human, or a combination of both which produces an effect of some kind) is neither a subject nor an object. Bennett's focus is not on what determines subjectivity so much as on discerning 'the active powers issuing from non subjects'.[35] Through this focus on action, Bennett develops the idea of an agency of assemblages, by which she means 'agency as a confederation of human and non-human elements'.[36] She argues that:

> bodies enhance their power *in* or *as a heterogeneous assemblage* [which means that the effectivity of agency] becomes distributed across an ontologically heterogeneous field, rather than being a capacity localised in a human body or in a collective produced (only) by human efforts.[37]

One of the examples Bennett gives of a heterogeneous assemblage is of a power grid which, understood broadly, includes electrons, trees, human (social, legal, linguistic) constructions, wire, people, fires, and so on.[38]

The idea that matter has its own vitality seems difficult or novel, Bennett argues, because we have

> deep cultural attachments to the ideas that matter is inanimate and that real agency belongs only to humans or to God, and by

---

32. Bennett, *Vibrant Matter*, 20.
33. Bennett, *Vibrant Matter*, 62.
34. Bennett, *Vibrant Matter*, 39–43.
35. Bennett, *Vibrant Matter*, ix.
36. Bennett, *Vibrant Matter*, 21.
37. Bennett, *Vibrant Matter*, 23.
38. Bennett, *Vibrant Matter*, 24–8.

> the need for an action-oriented perception that must overlook
> much of the swirling vitality of the world.[39]

Not with standing the prior theories of Diderot and Holbach, in addition to the thinkers whose ideas Bennett acknowledges as preceding her own (Spinoza, de Vries, Kant, Driesch and Bergson), the contrasting Newtonian-mechanistic understanding has been highly influential in Western Modern thinking, persuasively conveying the idea that matter is essentially passive or inert: hence the claims of vital materialism may well seem novel.[40] New materialism draws on current ideas such as the insights of theoretical physics over the last century in which 'forces, changes, waves, virtual particles and empty space suggest an ontology that is very different from the sub stantialist Cartesian or mechanistic Newtonian accounts of matter.'[41]

Vital materialism presents significant opportunities for re-thinking the way we understand human beings, matter, and the relationship between the two. It questions and begins to break down the dualistic binaries between human and other-than-human, between life and matter, insisting on making the boundaries between these categories less rigidly defined. This has ecological-political ramifications. As Bennett argues

---

39. Bennett, *Vibrant Matter*, 119. Despite the appearance of novelty, new materialisms are not entirely new but form part of the retrieval of 'the Real' in Continental philosophy. Christopher Baker, Thomas A James, and John Reader, *A Philosophy of Christian Materialism: Entangled Fidelities and the Public Good* (Farnham: Ashgate, 2015), 1. To some extent many new materialisms build on prior theories of matter, for example Diderot and Holbach posited a potentiality of energy within matter, speaking of 'the continual motion inherent in matter', Baron D'Holbach, *System of Nature, Volume 1* (Kitchener, Ontario: Batoche Books, 1868), 27.

40. Not only does vital materialism contest the Modernist claims which have mostly endorsed anthropocentric quarantines such as human-nature and matter-life, the new materialism's emphasis on the capacity of matter to be an 'actant' or operator also contests the post modern emphasis on reality as socially constructed, an idea which Michael Northcott sees as grounded in anthropocentrism. Michael S Northcott, *A Political Theology of Climate Change* (Grand Rapids: Eerdmans, 2013), 191.

41. Diana Coole and Samantha Frost, 'Introducing the New Materialisms', in *New Materialisms: Ontology, Agency, and Politics*, edited by Diana Coole and Samantha Frost (Durham: Duke University Presss, 2010), 12–13.

> the image of dead or thoroughly instrumentalised matter feeds human hubris and our earth-destroying fantasies of conquest and consumption. …The figures of an intrinsically in animate matter may be one of the impediments to the emergence of more ecological and more materially sustainable modes of production and consumption.[42]

By acknowledging a variety of other-than-human actants, the vital materialism posited by Bennett goes substantially beyond traditional discourse around 'the environment'. The concept of environmentalism is limited because it too often implies that human beings are the only true subjects and that we are surrounded by a passive environment which is not really part of us. Bennett says:

> If environmentalists are selves who live on earth, vital materialists are selves who live as earth, who are more alert to the capacities and limitations … of the various materials that they are.[43]

Although Bennett acknowledges that environmentalism has brought some benefits, she questions its ability to deal with the ideology of prosperity and consumption, positing vital materialism as a better way forward.[44] There are three advantages, argues Bennett, to adopting vital materialism over environmentalism: a) the term 'materiality' applies more horizontally to relations between human and other-than-human whereas environmentalism has meaning only in relation to human culture; b) vital materialism provides 'an alternative both to the idea of nature as a purposive, harmonious process and to the idea of nature as a blind mechanism';[45] c) it suggests that human flesh too has an 'alien' quality, and this can remind us 'of the very *radical* nature of the (fractious) kinship between the human and the non-human'.[46] Although environmentalism has 'raised good political questions' Bennett points out that vital materialism helps us to look

---

42. Bennett, *Vibrant Matter*, ix.
43. Bennett, *Vibrant Matter*, 111.
44. Bennett, *Vibrant Matter*, 110.
45. Bennett, *Vibrant Matter*, 112.
46. Bennett, *Vibrant Matter*, 112, italics in original.

more deeply at the force and effects of non-humans and the affinities between them and us.[47]

Bennett's claim that we are surrounded not by in animate matter but by heterogeneous assemblages more readily allows a topic such as the 1991 spilling and firing of oil in the Persian Gulf to be seen as an interconnected series of events and interactions. Part of Bennett's argument is to ask how patterns of consumption might change if we began to see 'garbage' as 'an accumulating pile of lively and potentially dangerous matter?'[48] Reflection on the images of burning oil in the Gulf War invites a similar question: how might our actions change if we see the spillage, even the extraction, of oil, whether as the consequence of the workings of our peace-time economy or as an act of war, as similarly involving something which is not only a resource/fuel for human consumption but also, like garbage, is 'lively and potentially dangerous'? It might challenge an automatic acceptance that oil is merely a useful but inert material, in capable of agency, that it exists as an object to be extracted, manipulated, bought, sold, and consumed by human agents, and that the present scale of mining and drilling is an inevitable and normal part of human enterprise and is therefore beyond critique.

Deep incarnation

Theology is constantly being reviewed and revised as it responds to new scientific, social and philosophical ideas. Changes in the understanding of the nature and meaning of matter are among the challenges and opportunities facing Christian thought today. The philosophical-political approach to matter taken by Jane Bennett and others tends to eschew religious expression. For Bennett, although matter 'is a force to be reckoned with' it is not 'purposive in any strong sense.'[49] Similarly, Diana Coole argues for 'a process of materialization and the nature of its fecundity … without relying on mysticisms

---

47. Bennett, *Vibrant Matter*, 111.
48. Bennett, *Vibrant Matter*, ix.
49. Bennett, *Vibrant Matter*, 62.

derived from animism, religion or romanticism'.[50] Nevertheless, despite their reservations about asserting new materialisms in conjunction with religion, Diana Coole and Samantha Frost implicitly create a space for religious discourse when they claim that in the ontology of new materialism 'there is no definitive break between sentient and non sentient entities or between material and spiritual phenomena'.[51] Because they break down rigid distinctions between life and matter, new materialisms provide a philosophical basis from which theologies might critique both neo-Platonic dualisms and the Modern mechanistic world view.

Anne Elvey engages with new and vital materialisms from the perspective of ecofeminist theology in order to re-think transcendence so that it is 'not (or not only) … outside matter', but is 'an otherness within (or proper to) the matter of Earth'.[52] Matter itself can be seen as self-transcendent and thereby capable of being oriented to, and mediating, the 'other' whether the other is some aspect of the material world and/or God.[53] This thinking, which connects with Plumwood's critique of hierarchical dualism, resonates with vital materialism when it questions the idea 'that Earth is without agency'.[54] The idea that Earth or matter may have a degree of agency and an ability to self-transcend assumes an ethos, and an ethic, which puts aside the idea that we adequately know the Earth 'other' and thereby can thoughtlessly utilise it. In terms of ecotheology, this understanding of materiality invites a 'turn toward the material otherness of an earth community' by adopting 'a stance of unknowing' about both nature and the divine.[55] This contests both the notion that transcendence is necessarily beyond the natural world and the dualistic framework that quarantines transcendence from immanence. It resonates with

---

50. Diana Coole, 'The Inertia of Matter and the Generativity of Flesh', in *New Materialisms: Ontology, Agency, and Politics*, edited by Diana Coole and Samantha Frost (Durham: Duke University Presss, 2010), 92.
51. Coole and Frost, 'Introducing the New Materialisms', 10.
52. Anne Elvey, 'Material Elements: The Matter of Women, the Matter of Earth, the Matter of God', in *Post-Christian Feminisms: A Critical Approach*, edited by Lisa Isherwood and Kathleen McPhilliips (Aldershot: Ashgate, 2008), 55.
53. Elvey, 'Material Elements', 53–55.
54. Anne Elvey, *The Matter of the Text: Material Engagements between Luke and the Five Senses* (Sheffield: Sheffield Phoenix Press, 2011), 8.
55. Elvey, 'Material Elements', 55.

the ecological claim that human beings share an interdependence and interrelatedness with Earth others.

The variety of new materialist discourse, and the hierarchical dualisms which they contest, show a degree of overlap with the political theology of Michael Northcott who attends to the environmentally detrimental impact of the Cartesian mind/body split, often identified as the intellectual marker of the Modern era. Northcott notes that from the time of Descartes and Newton, nature and society became separated, with nature becoming 'available for human control, dominion, and reordering'.[56] Cartesian/Newtonian understandings have been increasingly challenged in the twentieth century by new scientific understandings, and for Northcott these new understandings indicate a return to a more pre-Copernican type of 'relational cosmology'.[57] Northcott, like Bennett, uses Bruno Latour's idea of the existence of 'global actor networks' (various human parties) involved in climate change as well as a 'parliament of things'.[58] In his understanding of matter, Northcott goes beyond the theologically avoidant discourse of new materialism and echoes Elvey's ecofeminist approach when he seeks to articulate a non-anthropocentric theology which conjoins the material and the spiritual, a conjunction which he believes occurred in the Christian religion prior to the Modern era.

Northcott's fore shadowing of a less dichotomised relationship between humankind and matter is also found in the understanding of matter expressed in the ecologically significant idea of deep incarnation. The meaning of Jesus Christ is at the heart of Christian faith therefore the doctrine of the Incarnation is central for Christian thought. The doctrine is also important for theology which takes an ecological ethos seriously, because the base meaning of incarnation suggests that an intricate relationship exists between God and matter. Ecological theology tends to resist anthropocentric theological approaches, and in its discourse on the Incarnation it consequently tends to be critical of a predominantly human focus, wary of any suggestion that God's purpose and focus in the Incarnation was exclu-

---

56. Northcott, *A Political Theology of Climate Change*, 51, 190.
57. Northcott, *A Political Theology of Climate Change*, 51, 190.
58. Northcott, *A Political Theology of Climate Change*, 199, 193.

sively limited to the human.[59] The notion of deep incarnation moves towards precisely the kind of non-anthropocentric Christology which ecological theology seeks.

Niels Gregersen is the originator of the term 'deep incarnation', an idea which is becoming increasingly discussed in ecological theology.[60] The central claim of deep incarnation is that the event of Jesus Christ occurs so deeply within creation that a connection can be claimed not only between divine embodiment and other human beings but also between divine embodiment and other-then-human nature. God's enfleshment in Christ is understood to be 'deep' because it is 'an incarnation into the very tissue of biological existence, and system of nature'.[61] In deep incarnation the body of Jesus is seen as extensive, sharing not only biological and social existence with all human beings but with the rest of the created order: Jesus' body and mind (like our own bodies and minds) 'share the same conditions of metabolism and climate-dependence as any other living organism'.[62] To express the profundity of this connection, Gregersen draws on the concepts of deep ecology (humans are embedded within ecological systems) and deep history (which emphasises the things we share with animals and plants as part of our common ancestry).[63]

Deep incarnational theology resists anthropocentrism by downplaying the human aspect of the Incarnation in favour of asserting

---

59. Ecotheology tends to be 'characterised by the suspicion that an exclusive focus on human interests—whether in culture, the economy, politics or the church— forms one of the root causes of the widespread devastation of ecosystems', Ernst M. Conradie, *An Ecological Christian Anthropology: At Home on Earth?* (Aldershot: Ashgate, 2005), 96. Similarly, a sole or prime emphasis on Christ's relationship with human beings not only 'obscures Christ's prior relationship with all flesh and indeed with all created things', it has also resulted in a situation where 'books on Christology tend to avoid ecological themes, and books on ecotheology tend to avoid Christology', Duncan Reid, 'En fleshing the Human: An Earth-Revealing, Earth-Healing Christology', in *Earth Revealing—Earth Healing: Ecology and Christian Theology*, edited by Denis Edwards (Collegeville: Liturgical Press, 2001), 71.
60. Niels Gregersen, 'The Cross of Christ in an Evolutionary World', *Dialog: A Journal of Theology*, 40 (2001): 205.
61. Gregersen, 'The Cross of Christ in an Evolutionary World,' 205.
62. Niels Henrik Gregersen, 'Christology', in *Systematic Theology and Climate Change: Ecumenical Perspectives*, edited by Michael S Northcott and Peter M Scott (London: Routledge, 2014), 45.
63. Gregersen, 'Christology', 40.

correspondences between Jesus Christ and the broader world of nature and of all matter. Gregersen notes that even though Paul says that Christ was 'bearing human likeness' (Phil 2:7), the New Testament does not say that God became human *per se*, rather, that God took on flesh. In the Gospel of John, argues Gregersen, the divine Logos 'became flesh *(Sarx egeneto)* and was present in Jesus *as* flesh, *with* the flesh of others, and *for* flesh'; and in the person of Christ 'the divine Logos and the material *sarx* are co-present ...'.[64] Thus John's Gospel:

> uses a poly semantic concept of *sarx*, referring neutrally to the whole nexus of materiality: positively to the living and spirited embodiment, and negatively to the world of sin and decay. Accordingly ... [i]n Jesus Christ, the divine Logos assumed the entire realm of humanity, biological existence, earth and soil.[65]

This idea is similarly expressed by ecologically sympathetic biblical scholar Norman Habel who speaks of 'that piece of Earth called Jesus Christ'.[66]

Because Jesus Christ reveals the divine Logos through and in himself, he is able to hold all things (that is, all kinds of matter, living or otherwise) together '*within* the matrix of materiality that we share with other living beings'.[67] Because in deep incarnational theology Christology is necessarily embedded within a theology of creation, it means that instead of being seen only as a figure of history, Jesus Christ is to be seen as 'synchronous with each creature in time and co-inherent in all that exists in time and space'.[68] This theology resonates with the interrelationship between different types of matter asserted by vital materialism because it claims that rather than there being two distinct realities (God and nature) there is one complex

---

64. Gregersen, 'Christology', 45–6, italics in original.
65. Gregersen, 'Christology', 45.
66. Norman C Habel, 'Gospel and Creed, based on A Theology of Deep Incarnation and Reconciliation', Season of Creation, 6, <http://seasonofcreation. com/wp-content/uploads/2010/04/a-theology-of-deep-incarnation-and-reconciliation.pdf>. Accessed 26 November 2016.
67. Gregersen, 'Christology', 36.
68. Gregersen, 'Christology', 36.

reality.[69] That is to say, all things participate in God, and God and world are united in Christ.[70]

A deep incarnational approach questions exclusively human-centred understandings of Jesus' (and implicitly our own) genealogies. Gregersen goes beyond Jesus' human genealogies as presented by the Gospels of Matthew and Luke, utilising evolutionary understandings to claim 'the ancestral bonds of Jesus with other creatures'.[71] This approach suggests that we can move beyond the limitations of ourselves as only human and see ourselves also in other ways: as animals, vertebrates, carbon, matter, and so on.

The emphasis on materiality in the incarnational theology of Gregersen resonates with a number of other contributions to ecotheological discourse. Neil Darragh claims that 'Jesus of Nazareth ... is also a function in the carbon and oxygen cycles of the planet, a mammal, an event in the production-consumption processes of first century Palestine'.[72] Elizabeth Johnson claims that the solidarity of Jesus is with the whole created world.[73] For Denis Edwards, Jesus is 'the self-transcendence of the world of matter reaching out to God [in a way which is] identical with the absolute self-communication of God'.[74] Ernst Conradie argues that in contemporary concepts, the *sarx* of the Incarnation 'comprises the whole material universe from quarks to atoms in their manifold combinations and transformations through chemical and biological evolution'.[75]

The idea that Jesus has correspondence with all flesh, and with all matter, theologically affirms the importance of physicality and matter, raising its status in a way that contrasts with a number of earth-denying spiritualities which have at times emerged in the history of Christian thought. If matter is the locus of divine revelation, then an

---

69. Gregersen, 'Christology', 36–7.
70. But 'where the Son and the Spirit is, there is also the Father', Gregersen, 'Christology', 38.
71. Gregersen, 'Christology', 39.
72. Neil Darragh, 'Adjusting to the Newcomer: Theology and Ecotheology', *Pacifica*, 13/2 (2000): 171.
73. Elizabeth A Johnson, 'An Earthy Christology', *America* (2009): 28.
74. Denis Edwards, *Jesus and the Cosmos* (Mahwah: St Paul Publications, 1991), 83.
75. Ernst M Conradie (ed.), *Creation and Salvation: Volume 2: A Companion on Recent Theological Movements*, Studies in Religion and the Environment/Studien Zur Religion und Umwelt, vol. 2 (Berlin: LIT Verlag, 2012), 111.

inherent dignity and value can be ascribed not only to human beings but to the whole cosmos. As John of Damascus says, matter must be honoured 'because God has filled it with His grace and power'.[76] This world-affirming attitude is important for an ecological ethos both because it claims that the material world is inherently (rather than merely instrumentally) valuable and because it suggests that environmental restoration and healing may be part of God's purpose for the world. A theology which emphasises the organic and material dimension of the Incarnation is coherent with much of the Christian tradition. Even though the centrality of matter has at times been eclipsed by an over-emphasis on the spiritual, matter occupies a highly significant place within the Christian narrative and tradition. The tangible nature of Christian Sacraments, the bodily actions of healing and feeding in Jesus' ministry, Jesus' bodily death and Resurrection, and the image of the Church as the body of Christ indicate the primacy of body, flesh and matter in Christianity, a faith which some have identified as 'The Religion of the Incarnation'.[77]

Like vital materialism, deep incarnational theology implicitly transcends hierarchical dualisms and asserts stronger connections between spirit and matter, also between life and matter. In the Incarnation God entered the world in a new way and continues to be present with the whole of creation, not only with humankind but with ecosystems and with the entire biosphere. In this way Christ is representative of the universe as well as humanity and thereby unifies all that is.

Deep incarnation presents a theological understanding that we are intricately connected with the material world. Humans are both profoundly reliant on it for our survival as well as able to radically influence its working—for example through the violence we inflict in the process of war and the (at times equal) violence which is

---

76. St John of Damascus, *On the Divine Images: Three Apologies against Those Who Attack the Divine Images*, translated by David Anderson (Crestwood, NY: St Vladimir's Seminary Press, 2000), 23.

77. In 1889 the sub-title of *Lux Mundi* was given as 'A Series of Studies in the Religion of the Incarnation'. Charles Gore (editor), *Lux Mundi: A Series of Studies in the Religion of the Incarnation* (London: John Murray, 1889). In more recent decades, and in a more self-consciously ecotheological vein, Sallie McFague said that Christianity is '*par excellence* the religion of the incarnation'. Sallie McFague, *The Body of God: An Ecological Theology* (Minneapolis: Fortress, 1993), 163.

entailed in what we have come to think of as our 'ordinary' economic-commercial-industrial activity. Today we understand, in a way that was not available to the ancient world, that our actions (for example emitting high levels of carbon or spilling oil) impact the lives of other people, of creatures of all kinds, and of ecosystems. Awareness of the commonalities we share with other creatures, even with the physical composition of the entire universe, invites a theological re-imaging of our human identity in closer communion with other entities of Earth. It also opens the possibility of human beings adopting a humbler approach to the world of nature. Humility belies anthropocentrism, taking our focus beyond species or individual hubris to the reality of the more-than-human world. As Elvey has noted, ecologically-related events such as the 2009 bush fires in Victoria can invite a greater humility, 'a kind of kenosis, which has theological import in terms of its capacity to turn us toward the reality of our situation'.[78]

Conclusion

The *Ecological Aspects of War* project, which was the genesis of the essays in this collection, has sought to identify and explore the links between complex and interlaced categories such as: war and peace, human beings and the natural world, ecology and religion, violence and religion. This essay has explored one possible way of making some connections. Brauer's argument that peace can be at least as detrimental as war for the other-than-human parts of the natural world exposes the way that our peace-time economic and commercial enterprise is grounded in a degree of anthropocentrism that has become increasingly untenable in the present ecological context. Expressions of violence and destruction involving the more-than-human world such as occurred in 1991 in the Persian Gulf are indicative of anthropocentric dualisms—including that of life versus matter—that too sharply separate human beings from the natural world, from which we have evolved and on which we rely for our physical existence and well-being.

---

78. Anne Elvey, 'Ashes and Dust: On (Not) Speaking About God Ecologically', in *Eco-Theology*, edited by Elaine Wainwright, Luiz Carlos Susin and Felix Wilfred, *Concilium* 3 (2009): 39.

Vital materialism poses a significant ecological and philosophical challenge to an unequivocal demarcation between humans and other-than-humans and between life and matter: the claim of Bennett and others that matter can self-transform, self-organise and itself exercise agency challenges the notions that only humans are subjects or agents and that matter is necessarily to be understood as non-agential, inert and passive. More specifically, the idea that non-human materialities are to be seen as participants rather than objects poses a radical challenge to the anthropocentric imaginary which has dominated the modern industrial and technological era and has negatively impacted entities and ecosystems on a global scale.

The re-thinking of matter which occurs in vital materialism has resonances with the theology of deep incarnation where a non-anthropocentric Christology takes the emphasis off Jesus of Nazareth as human in favour of seeing him in a wider biophysical category, inviting us to revision both God and ourselves as embedded in and related to the entire Earth community. Theologies of matter such as deep incarnation respond to the recovery, called for by Northcott, of 'the primitive sense of an interconnection between nature, society, and the sacred'.[79]

Ecological questions of our time, including those relating to oil extraction, usage and spills, are highly relevant to the kind of philosophical and theological reflection given by Bennett, Northcott, Gregersen and others. Bennett asks:

> What would happen to our thinking about nature if we experienced materialities as actants, and how would the direction of public policy shift if it attended more carefully to their trajectories and powers?[80]

Her question invites reflection on the meaning of oil itself as an actant which is part of the wider cosmos in which the divine has become deeply embedded through the event of the Incarnation.

Vital materialism and the matter-affirming theology of deep incarnation expand our philosophical and theological vision of the material world. Oil, like other forms of matter, acquires a broader

---

79. Northcott, *A Political Theology of Climate Change*, 193.
80. Bennett, *Vibrant Matter*, 62.

meaning and is seen as interwoven not only with the human world (economics, politics, war and peace) but also with the ecological (it is an actant which is able to radically alter the biota and ecosystems of the Persian Gulf and of the world) and with the divine 'other' (who in deep incarnational theology is understood to be deeply embedded in the more-than-human world). This provides a broader basis for understanding some of the ecological aspects of war and invites critique of the anthropocentric practice (both in times of peace and war) of extracting and utilising the dynamic and lively fossil fuels embedded in Earth.

Bonhoeffer and 'The Right to Self Assertion': Understanding Theologically the Mastery of Nature and War

Dianne Rayson

Introduction

A short series of lectures in February, 1932, was coordinated by the student chaplain of Charlottenburg-Berlin Technical College, the twenty-six-year-old Dietrich Bonhoeffer. By this time, Bonhoeffer had written two dissertations, been to Union Theological Seminary in New York, and met Karl Barth. He had commenced his ecumenical work with the World Alliance and, importantly, was already critiquing the rise of German National Socialism and the prevailing world view of *Kulturprotestantismus* (loosely, cultural Protestantism) regarding the validity and supremacy of the nation state, including the role of Christian action in that context.

His own lecture in this series was titled 'The Right to Self-Assertion'. It constitutes the exposure of a theme that would recur through his Finkenwalde seminary teaching and in his major work, *Ethics*, and would have been at the core of his final, unfinished (and lost) manuscript. That theme is self-assertion: the rights of humans and the associated problem of the assertion of rights over against those of others. Bonhoeffer challenges us to consider the historical-social responsibility that is required of Christian action in the concrete world.

In this essay, I argue that a valid extension of Bonhoeffer's thesis enables us to understand 'self-assertion' as the underlying problem not only of the violence of war, Bonhoeffer's position, but also the broader issue of violence to the ecology. The two, war and nature, are linked most obviously in terms of collateral damage and exploiting one for the other, whereby the environment suffers from the warfare itself (consider the image of the destroyed battlefields of World War 1) or is used as a weapon (for example, poisoning water sources, burning vegetation cover) but they are also fundamentally connected at a conceptual level where theological interrogation of mastery, power and violence can occur. Such interrogation constitutes the purpose of this discussion.

The immediate context for Bonhoeffer's lecture was the mass unemployment in Germany which had just reached its zenith at over thirty percent. Having suffered the tragic carnage of World War 1, Germany's social conditions during the inter-war period were by then resulting in runaway inflation and unemployment of over six million workers.[1] Bonhoeffer was aware of the demoralising effect of unemployment, but also that being *employed* under these conditions sets up a similar uncertainty of dispensability, or what he describes as 'the superfluous human existence', and *dahinvegetieren*—a vegetative existence. This is seen in the following, when he asks:

> What right do you have to assert yourself in the struggle for human existence, in full awareness that you are thereby ruining, destroying, and leaving the lives of others prey to meaninglessness? Stand up for your rights! Or surrender them![2]

Bonhoeffer is both acknowledging the immediate situation of his student audience and the implied wider audience of both employed and unemployed. In doing so, he sets up the larger questions concerning not only individual rights but those of communities, nations, and humanity at large. This critique of the rights of the employed at the expense of the unemployed becomes but one component of Bonhoeffer's larger project concerning the critique of industrialisation. It is in this context that the key issues of mastery of technology and mastery of nature are framed. The attempted mastery of technology and nature forms the core of Bonhoeffer's lecture and therefore underpins

---

1. Dietrich Bonhoeffer, Ecumenical, Academic, and Pastoral Work: 1931–1932 (DBWE 11), edited by Victoria J Barnett, Mark S Brocker, and Michael B Lukens, translated by Anne Schmidt-Lange, et al., (Minneapolis: Fortress, 2012), FN 4, 247. All Bonhoeffer quoted is from Dietrich Bonhoeffer Works, English Edition, Vol. 1–16, edited by Victoria J Barnett, Barbara Wodjhoski and Clifford J Green.
2. Dietrich Bonhoeffer, Ecumenical, Academic, and Pastoral Work: 1931–1932 (DBWE 11), 248; Christoph Strohm, 'Editor's After word to the German Edition', in Bonhoeffer, DBWE 11, 477.

this essay. It also serves as a platform for considering attempted mastery as a contributing factor to anthropogenic climate disruption.

Two responses to the question

Bonhoeffer posits that there have traditionally been two answers to the question of self-assertion, or the 'fundamental question of all life',[3] that is, survival: these are, namely, the Eastern and Western responses characterised broadly by 'surrender' and 'mastery' respectively.

Framing his argument in this way reflects Bonhoeffer's strong interest in Eastern religions and in Gandhi's application of personal faith to political and social responses. Bonhoeffer was hoping to visit and study with Gandhi, whom he saw as presenting an authentic response to Christ's challenges. He had made three attempts to do so, the third in 1939 when he chose instead to return to Germany to stand with the church and his nation through the war. Bonhoeffer would later write of Gandhi that he represented a more solid form of Christianity and community life than that which he saw in much of the Christian church of Germany. Colleagues remember Bonhoeffer as thinking that 'Gandhi thought more highly of The Sermon on the Mount than most Christians' and wondering whether Gandhi didn't represent 'God's will for the nations'.[4]

In what Bonhoeffer calls the Eastern response to the fundamental question, he refers to:

> the distant, fertile, sunny, form- and idea-rich world of India,
> in which the body is easily provided with good things and
> thus the soul is left free for surrender and self-deepening.[5]

The interrelatedness of humanity with the rest of the biosphere is a Jain notion which also appears in the Hindu Upanishad as *tat tva-masi*, meaning that one's true self or essence is identical with the whole of existence.[6] The culturally Hindu Gandhi had been mentored in Jainism and acknowledged both belief systems as being influential,

---

3. Bonhoeffer, DBWE 11, 250.
4. Bonhoeffer, Barcelona, Berlin, New York, edited by Clifford J Green, translated by Douglas W Stott, (Minneapolis: Fortress, 2008), FN 183, 50.
5. Bonhoeffer, DBWE 11, 250.
6. Bonhoeffer, DBWE 11, FN 15, 250.

in addition to his reading of Christianity that had occurred largely in London. Bonhoeffer uses *tat tvamasi* to describe the way the (Eastern) soul breathes the life and cycles around it, 'probing and pondering its rhythm and depths, which are basically the depths of the soul itself . . . In this way the submerging soul recognizes itself again in all that lives, as if in thousands of mirrors; out of every form of nature it hears the quiet answer: *tat tvamasi*, this is you, you yourself'.[7]

Bonhoeffer presents this as an Eastern ontology and so the empirical response follows:

> the eternal awe of the sanctity of all life comes over the soul. It aches if nature suffers from violence; it is torn apart when living things are injured. You should not kill, for life is the soul, and life is you yourself; you should not do violence to any living thing; you should resist and reject anything in you that stimulates you to get your way with violence.[8]

In this, Bonhoeffer is outlining the Jain and Hindu commitment to non-violence as the manifestation of an interrelated ontology. The three jewels of Jainism: right faith, right conduct and right knowledge, are underpinned by personal practices of which non-violence, *ahimsa,* is one. This Jain discipline requires not simply removing non-violent actions from one's life, but removing the *ability* to commit violence, and, furthermore, removing the ability even to *conceive* of it. Violence toward the natural world would be a violation of the life force present there and also, by extension, a violation of oneself.[9] Violence can be understood here in its broadest sense of the assertion of power: Hannah Arendt recognised violence as both the flagrant manifestation of power and also a 'kind of mitigated power'.[10] Power denies the absolute autonomy of the other for the purposes (intended or unintended) of the perpetrator. In a world view which acknowledges the *jiva*, or the life force, throughout the entire cosmos, violence, or the direction of power, over humans, other species, or Earth

---

7. Bonhoeffer, DBWE 11, 250.
8. Bonhoeffer, DBWE 11, 251.
9. Agustín Pániker, Jainism: History, Society, Philosophy and Practice (New Delhi: Motilal Banarsidass, 2010).
10. Hannah Arendt, On Violence (San Diego: Harcourt Brace Jovanovich, 1970), 38.

herself, is contrary to the sanctity of life and therefore jeopardises one's own holiness.[11]

Gandhi's master stroke, according to Bonhoeffer, was in taking the notion of non-violence as it relates to the individual dealing with the universe, encapsulated in the individual, and expanding it to evoke community action and responsibility: non-violent (neither 'passive' nor 'pacifist') political resistance, *satyagraha*, classically demonstrated at the massacre of Amritsar in 1919. 'Placing the community under the commandment' of not destroying life and suffering in preference to any violence[12] Bonhoeffer saw both a rejection of the Western approach of violent struggle and a manifestation of the Sermon on the Mount, a text that Bonhoeffer and Gandhi both studied and responded to throughout their careers. Bonhoeffer would return again and again to the Sermon on the Mount, especially through his seminary teaching at Finkenwalde and in the section in *Ethics* on self-assertion.[13] Gandhi appeared to return to the Sermon on the Mount, as did Bonhoeffer, at the most crucial times in their lives when political action presented as an imperative.

Bonhoeffer presents the notion of an alternative, non-violent suffering as a contrast with the historical German/Western tradition of war and violence, whilst acknowledging Gandhi as a truer exemplification of the Christian ideal than what he saw emerging at home. The Eastern commitment to non-violence means that, rather than assert oneself, the individual learns to suffer, and ultimately die, and thus remains holy. Bonhoeffer uses the image of rural India with the presumed proximity to Earth and sustainable provision of needs inspiring an inherent sanctity for life. This may be an over-simplification reflecting, in part, the Orientalist thinking of the time[14] but was intended nonetheless to inspire a German audience that was devoid of hope and hardly interested in the notion of more suffering. Freedom *for* suffering would constitute Bonhoeffer's final proposition:

---

11. Christopher Key Chapple, 'Jainism, Ethics and Ecology,' in Bulletin for the Study of Religion, 39/2 (2010).
12. Bonhoeffer, DBWE 11, 251.
13. Bonhoeffer, 'History and Good', Ethics [DBWE 6], edited by Clifford J Green, translated by Reinhard Krauss, Charles C West, and Douglas W Stott (Minneapolis: Fortress, 2005), 239–45.
14. Alessandra Marino, 'The Tomb of Orientalism? Europe after the Lure of the East', in Third Text, 27/2 (2013).

this does not constitute acquiescence in order to protect one's holiness, but a turning toward the other and standing in their place as vicarious representative action.[15] This notion will be pursued below. First, however, I turn to the Western condition.

The West and the mastery of nature

Where Indians have learnt to 'suffer for the sake of the soul', Europeans have attempted to 'master nature in order to force it into their service'.[16] Bonhoeffer sees 'this position of human mastery over nature [as] the fundamental theme of European-American history'.[17] That is, Western history is characterised by an attempt to master and dominate both people (self-assertion which manifests ultimately as war) and, importantly, nature (emerging, at least in part in the West, as industrialisation).

Bonhoeffer portrays the Western apprehension of nature as a 'love/hate' relationship. On the one hand, the Romantics (both Early and Late) philosophically refocused our natural biophilia: humans' love of the aesthetic which nature bestows, the notion of perceived harmony, and validation of the emotional response to the outdoors.[18] Nonetheless, the Western relationship is marred by its innate tendency to assert power and become nature's enemy. Therefore, despite 'loving' nature, we 'hate' it and resent its untameable aspects. We simultaneously love it for its service to us through provision, its aesthetics, and even because it forces us to struggle against it in order to receive from it, eliciting a kind of respect for a worthy opponent whilst at the same

---

15. For a concise introduction to this key concept of Bonhoeffer's, see Clifford J. Green, 'Editor's Introduction to the English Edition', in Sanctorum Communio: A Theological Study of the Sociology of the Church (DBWE 1) (Minneapolis: Fortress, 1998); Bonhoeffer: A Theology of Sociality, revised edition (Grand Rapids: Wm B Eerdmans, 1999).

16. John A Moses, The Reluctant Revolutionary: Dietrich Bonhoeffer's Collision with Prusso-German History (New York: Berghahn Books, 2009), 93.

17. Bonhoeffer, DBWE 11, 252.

18. Karl Ameriks, 'Introduction: Interpreting German Idealism', in The Cambridge Companion to German Idealism, edited by Karl Ameriks, (Cambridge: Cambridge University Press, 2000); Dieter Sturma, 'Politics and the New Mythology: The Turn to Late Romanticism', in The Cambridge Companion to German Idealism, edited by Karl Ameriks, (Cambridge: Cambridge University Press, 2000).

time striving to control, overpower, and ultimately destroy it. Bonhoeffer surmises, 'the human path to nature is a broken one'.[19]

So, in contrast with the (possibly idealised) East, where humans apparently live with nature symbiotically, experiencing blessing and validating its life force, in the West, the coexistence is defined by struggle and premised on separation. Wendell Berry articulates this separation as follows:

> The contempt for the world or the hatred of it, that is exemplified by the wish to exploit it for the sake of cash and by the willingness to despise it for the sake of 'salvation,' has reached a terrifying climax in our own time. The rift between soul and body, the Creator and Creation, has admitted the entrance into the world of the machinery of the world's doom.[20]

However, Bonhoeffer cautions against the superficial preference of the Eastern over the Western approach to nature, identifying that in *both* solutions 'the human being steps outside the connection to nature and is something utterly different from an animal'.[21] His argument here is that, in contrast with the animals that live in accordance with the rhythms and laws of nature, humanity—both Eastern and Western—stands facing nature, 'ruling and conquering it'.[22] In the East, it is through suffering for the sake of the soul but, in the West, it is through the attempted mastery of nature. There is universality in the confrontation with nature, both an Eastern and Western challenge, despite the different manifestation of that confrontation, as Bonhoeffer sees it.

The contention between humans and nature also pertains to primal cultures when they transition to modern living and supersede traditional methods of land use. We have no evidence of any society, given population, affluence and technological increase (markers of

---

19. Bonhoeffer, DBWE 11, 252.
20. Cited in Steven Bouma-Prediger, The Greening of Theology: Ecological Models of Rosemary Radford Ruether, Joseph Sittler and Jürgen Moltmann, American Academy of Religion Series (Atlanta: Scholars, 1995), 1.
21. Bonhoeffer, DBWE 11, 252.
22. Bonhoeffer, DBWE 11, 252.

The Great Acceleration from around 1950 onwards)[23] which has not spiralled into destruction of the environment as a manifestation of the fundamental rupture in its relationship with nature. Accelerated increase in the three vital facets of population, affluence and technology characterise the key shift in humanity's global relationship with Earth and can be seen as marking the beginning of the geological epoch, named here as the Anthropocene. The human enterprise is the key driver of Earth System impact with the disastrous results of breaching Planetary Boundaries which have provoked climate disruption.[24]

In relevance to the above disruption, Bonhoeffer suggests that, 'fighting against it', forcing it 'to his service' both *catalogues* Western history, and *explains* a history characterised by war.[25] Attempted mastery of nature, machines, and ultimately other people, are dysfunctional attempts to respond to the key question of self-assertion. Bonhoeffer states that the Western 'solution' to the problem of survival, or self-assertion, is as a history of war, understood as a chronicle of violence, power and struggle. Here, war and the machine—technology—become conflated as the Western way of addressing the problem of self-assertion in society. The machine should be expected, or hoped at least, to make war *less* of an option: increasing technology should act as a deterrent and decrease the likelihood of violence; additionally, in the event of war, technology would be expected to limit carnage and the impact on the environment if humanity truly mastered it.

Instead, humanity thinks it masters technology but the machine actually masters humanity. The killing machine which was World War 1 had inflicted atrocities that, in Bonhoeffer's description, were 'impossible'[26] or unimaginable. The victim was universal: combatants, humanity, other species, Earth herself. 'Impossibility' implies the entrenched nature of the tendency to attempt mastery of others and hence the inevitability of violence and destruction. The continu-

---

23. Will Steffen et al., 'The Trajectory of the Anthropocene: The Great Acceleration', in The Anthropocene Review, 2/1 (2015).
24. Johan Rockström et al., 'A Safe Operating Space for Humanity', in Nature, 461/7263 (2009).
25. Bonhoeffer, DBWE 11, 255.
26. Bonhoeffer, DBWE 11, 255.

ing history of war throughout the twentieth and now into the twenty-first century demonstrates the environmental and ecological damage that war actualises: as an instance, consider Vietnam's Agent Orange and the burning oil fields of Kuwait as graphic examples. Robert Hirst reflected this in 'Mountains of Burma':

> Pack your bags full of guns and ammunition Bills fall due for the industrial revolution Scorch the earth till the earth surrenders.[27]

After World War 2, the Geneva Convention outlawed the destruction of dams, dykes and nuclear plants in war, but only if it threatened civilian life.[28] Targeting of sites with the potential of 'releasing dangerous forces' is now prohibited in so far as human life is considered to be at risk. Other species and ecosystems are not similarly protected in their own right. The Convention which protects against 'environmental modification techniques', that is, 'the deliberate manipulation of natural processes—the dynamics, composition or structure of the Earth, including its biota, lithosphere, hydrosphere and atmosphere, or of outer space'[29] in warfare has, as its purpose, the protection of human life. In fact, it is possible that as warfare has become 'safer' for humans, it has become even more dangerous to Earth. That is, as militaries target industrial features rather than face armies in direct conflict, the risk of contamination to the environment may increase. Technology has mastered humanity where human life is prioritised over other species, ecosystems and atmosphere but potentially finds itself at risk in the medium and long term from the effects of that very warfare.

The domination of technology over humanity also makes possible the 'subjugation of nature to human beings'.[30] Humanity, instead of 'having *dominion* over' birds, fish and animals,[31] has rather *dominated*

---

27. Robert Hirst, 'Mountains of Burma', on *Blue Sky Mining*, by Midnight Oil (Sony/ATV Music, 1990).
28. 'Protocol Additional to the Geneva Conventions of 12 August 1949, and Relating to the Protection of Victims of International Armed Conflicts (Protocol I)', Article 56.
29. 'Convention on the Prohibition of Military or Any Hostile Use of Environmental Modification Techniques' in *U.N.T.S.I.-17119*.
30. Bonhoeffer, *DBWE* 11, 255.
31. Gen 1:26

and ultimately harmed the entire Earth System[32] and this through the misguided use of technology. 'Mastery of the machine' becomes a trope for industrialised society. Capitalism, as historically played out in the West, had not resulted in less violence, let alone brought peace in Bonhoeffer's time. Capitalism as a human system has been complicit in the violence against Earth by regarding the resources of Earth as 'limitless', the environment simply a backdrop to core economic activity, and not placing economic penalties on waste or pollution.[33] Other systems may be similarly critiqued.

When machines are used for the purpose of killing and extending national boundaries, the result is catastrophic. The machine is 'placed in the deliberate service of destroying human life' but, instead, 'directs this fight primarily not against the human being but against nature'.[34] This had never been as evident as in World War 1. The result of technology's mastery of humanity means that humanity is left to live 'according to the machine's reality',[35] that is, in a world defined by technology and far removed from the close connection to nature typified in Eastern religions[36] and, in recent times, affirmed as natural by neuroscience and elements of physiological anthropology.[37] Ultimately, rather than being masters of either technology or of nature, humans are themselves mastered by both and rendered simply a shell of the humanity that is their destiny under God.

The ultimate violence against nature consists of the emerging threat of geo-engineering: war against Earth 'itself' in order to, ostensibly, protect it from itself. Reliance on geo-engineered interventions to limit the results of our human-driven changes to the Earth System is not only cynical but indicates an ill-founded commitment to human

---

32. Rockström et al., 'A Safe Operating Space'.
33. Carl Folke et al., 'Reconnecting to the Biosphere', *Ambio* 40 (2011); Naomi Klein, *This Changes Everything: Capitalism vs the Climate* (London: Allen Lane, 2014).
34. Bonhoeffer, *DBWE* 11, 255.
35. Bonhoeffer, *DBWE* 11, 255.
36. Including Israel's experience of belonging to the land as portrayed in the Hebrew Bible, and incidentally, also in primal spiritualities such as that of Indigenous Australians. See also Mary Evelyn Tucker and John A Grim, editors, *World views and Ecology: Religion, Philosophy and the Environment* (Maryknoll, NY: Orbis, 1994).
37. Jeffrey M Craig, Alan C Logan, and Susan L Prescott, 'Natural Environments, Nature Relatedness and the Ecological Theater: Connecting Satellites and Sequencing to Shinrin-Yoku', *Journal of Physiological Anthropology*, 35/1 (2016).

mastery where none actually exists. As Earth endures the sixth mass extinction—the first caused by the human species[38]—humans continue the use of violence against Earth herself in an attempt to protect the viability of the human species alone in the face of the climate crisis. The hypocrisy of this strategy is profound. The rejection of the rights of other species, and indeed, Earth Systems and ecologies and their subjugation to the assertion of the human species means that we now face such biodiversity loss that our own viability is at stake.[39] Using Bonhoeffer's analysis, geo-engineering might represent the ultimate manifestation of the machine mastering humanity and forcing us to live according to the rules of technology.

Reconciling these problems

The Right to Self-Assertion is the right to life, using power in a struggle over nature and others. The outrage that humans inevitably feel over nature and each other, what Bonhoeffer describes as their 'destiny',[40] can only be resolved when the notion of responsibility is brought to bear. In the context of the Nazification of Germany and Hitler's plans for border extension, there was an increasing currency developing around the notion of responsibility to the *Volk* or fellow nationals. This implied the responsibility to die for country.

Bonhoeffer challenges this notion. Responsibility, according to him, certainly leaves open the potential to lay down one's life, however, not 'the death of self-destruction, but rather to the freedom to sacrifice'. Motivation here is crucial: 'not for the glorification of personality but as sacrifice for brother'. In addressing the immediate political context, Bonhoeffer also provides a principle for the flourishing of human life, that 'life itself must be open to death', for only when life is understood 'from the perspective of death'[41] is the answer to the problem of self-

---

38. Gerardo Ceballos et al., 'Accelerated Modern Human-Induced Species Losses: Entering the Sixth Mass Extinction', in *Science Advances* 1/5 (2015).
39. Ceballos et al., 'Accelerated Modern Human-Induced Species Losses: Entering the Sixth Mass Extinction'; Elias Lazarus et al., 'Biodiversity Loss and the Ecological Footprint of Trade' in *Diversity*, 7/2 (2015).
40. Bonhoeffer, *DBWE* 11, 253.
41. Bonhoeffer, *DBWE* 11, 254.

assertion found. Instead of winning life by *killing*, true freedom and true humanity could only be asserted through *dying*:

> Humanity is responsible for its right to life, and it exercises this responsibility only where it sees that it too only lives from being able to die, from death, from sacrifice . . . The end . . . is the readiness for this deed, for sacrifice.[42]

The readiness for the deed of sacrifice for the fellow human being, according to Bonhoeffer, is the fullness of humanity, reflecting that fullness of humanity to be found in Christ's life, lived 'in the shadow or in the light of Golgotha. Because he was free to die, therefore he could live . . . His death sanctifies our life.'[43] Just as God, in God's freedom chose to be bound 'to historical human beings' through Christ,[44] in Christ, then, the human is emancipated and sanctified.

The human is not destined to simply struggle against nature and humanity, but, being free to death, is able to fully live. Bonhoeffer's conclusion that 'God is not free from them, but free for them' underpins his notion of both humanity's ontology—what it means to be fully human, and the ethic of being free for the sake of the other. Given Bonhoeffer's articulation of the problem of self-assertion, and his conclusion that viewing life from the perspective of death is the way to freedom for other, and the way humans might flourish, what might this contribute to an ecoethical response to the climate crisis we now face? As Bonhoeffer spoke to his signal issue of Nazism, how could his insights be applied to the contemporary signal issue of war against Earth herself?

In the immediate context, Bonhoeffer challenged his original audience to resist asserting power over others despite the volatile, uncertain times and attempted to frame that of which he was already apprehensive, namely, the rise of Nazism and the leadership

---

42. Bonhoeffer, *DBWE* 11, 256.
43. Bonhoeffer, *DBWE* 11, 256.
44. Bonhoeffer, *Act and Being: Transcendental Philosophy and Ontology in Systematic Theology* (*DBWE* 2), edited by Wayne Whitson Floyd Jr, translated by H Martin Rumscheidt (Minneapolis: Fortress, 1998), 90.

of Hitler.[45] It is Christ's *kenosis* (self-emptying) that challenges the assertion of rights in all forms: to employment, over Jews, Hitler's vision of expansionism, assertion of rights as an individual or as a nation: all these are brought into focus by Bonhoeffer through the ethic of *Stellvertretung*, vicarious action on behalf of or in the place of the other.[46]

By extension then, sacrifice on behalf of other species and Earth herself is implied as the way humanity best expresses its assertion for survival. Coupled with Bonhoeffer's notion of one unified reality,[47] so that in Christ 'one embraces both God and the world, never God or the world',[48] what emerges is an ethic that responds to nature and humanity, not in struggle for domination or attempt at mastery, but in mutual sacrifice. Only in this freedom is humanity able to fully live on behalf of the other. As we see sacrifice in the natural world as a matter of course, in the food chains, life cycles and ecosystems, so too humanity must begin to see itself as a component of an Earth System based in sacrifice.[49]

A life 'abiding in love', Bonhoeffer wrote in his first thesis, rather than in the violence of the struggle for power, 'breaks continuity with the historical process'.[50] 'Breaking continuity' with the processes of biodiversity loss and the breaching of other Earth boundaries, all of which contribute to the climate catastrophe and signify the consequences of humanity's persistence of self-assertion, is not simply

---

45. A year later Bonhoeffer would have his radio lecture, 'The Führer and the Individual in the Younger Generation' cut short in broadcast, and only months later would have penned the essay 'The Church and the Jewish Question', Bonhoeffer, *DBWE* 11, 268, 361. In these, he was among the very first to publicly oppose Hitler's authority and strategy.
46. See, for example, 'The Structure of Responsible Life', in Bonhoeffer, *DBWE* 6, 257–88.
47. See, for example, Bonhoeffer, *DBWE* 2.
48. Geffrey B Kelly, 'Editor's Introduction to the English Edition' in Bonhoeffer, *Discipleship*, translated by Barbara Green and Reinhard Krauss (Minneapolis: Fortress, 2001).
49. The eco-feminist, Val Plumwood, writes of becoming personally aware of the significance of the notion of food chain and humanity's part in it when she was attacked by a saltwater crocodile in Australia. Val Plumwood, *The Eye of the Crocodile* (Canberra: Australian National University e Press, 2012), at <http://press.anu.edu.au? p=208511>. Accessed 16 April 2015.
50. Bonhoeffer, *DBWE* 1, 146.

desirable in order to flourish as fully human, but is a matter of existential necessity. As it characterises the true church, 'vicarious representative action is the life-principle of the new humanity' in Christ.[51] To what extent is the new humanity prepared to break continuity and embark on a life 'abiding in love'? What does that look like for the globalised community of the twenty-first century, constrained both geopolitically and by the dominance of a capitalist system underpinned by multinational companies which in turn transcend the nation state?[52] One is reminded here of Bonhoeffer's well known maxim that it is not enough 'just to bind up the wounds of the victims beneath the wheel but to seize the wheel itself'.[53]

Sacrifice on behalf of others in the context of planetary boundary breaching and climate disruption demands that we re-assess the human obligation, not only to the human victims of climate change, of which there are already millions and there will be many more, as coastal land is reclaimed by rising seas, worsening storms and fires increase their destructive capabilities, and food in security increases. As direct effects of climate change take hold, the potential for political and social systems to collapse and pre-empt their own sequelae increases and all evidence indicates that it is the poorest and least responsible for carbon pollution who are the most vulnerable to these impacts.[54]

In this generation, it may, to some extent, mean taking an even *more* anthropocentric philosophical approach[55] to our relationship with Earth so that the responsibility that humans must accept for creating the problem of climate catastrophe is acknowledged and dealt with, at a minimum, by taking commensurate responsibility for its

---

51. Bonhoeffer, *DBWE* 1, 147.

52. Andrea Tornielli and Giacomo Galeazzi, *This Economy Kills: Pope Francis on Capitalism and Social Justice*, translated by Demetrio S Yocum (Collegeville, MN: Liturgical, 2015); Klein, *This Changes Everything*.

53. Bonhoeffer, *Berlin: 1932-1933* (*DBWE 12 B*), edited by Larry L Rasmussen, translated by Isabel Best (Minneapolis: Fortress, 2009), 367.

54. Alistair Woodward et al., 'Protecting Human Health in a Changing World: The Role of Social and Economic Development', *Bulletin of the World Health Organization* 78/9 (2000); United Nations, *United Nations Framework Convention on Climate Change* (Geneva, 1992).

55. Clive Hamilton, 'Opinion: A New Kind of Human Being. Reply to Steve Fuller,' at <www.abc.net.au/religion/articles/2015/09/17/ 4314453.htm>. Accessed 21 September 2015.

potential effects and management. As Larry Rasmussen puts it, 'We have no ethic on the books or in existing moral theory that assigns responsibility in keeping with such far-flung consequences of human action.'[56] But Bonhoeffer's vicarious representative action implies taking on guilt and suffering for climate change regardless of our perceived personal culpability. The task at hand is to imagine what that suffering on behalf of the Earth community might entail. Surely a new examination of social and financial structures which are dependent upon fossil fuels, exist for the financial benefit of shareholders, and result ultimately in climate injustice (for example, through natural disasters, people losing their homes, food and water scarcity) is a start.[57] It would seem that the excessive consumption and structural violence[58] that characterises this age would have to be challenged, just as we must prepare for suffering both as an inevitable consequence but also, according to Bonhoeffer, as a positive result of 'being' church. Ultimately, there is no 'being-free-from' the problem of climate change without humanity and (specifically) the church 'being-free-for' each other[59] and, in this context, for the whole of the Earth community.

Finally, what of 'seizing the wheel itself',[60] Bonhoeffer's metaphor for dismantling the underlying cause of the problem? Bonhoeffer's challenge to this generation, and those who follow, will require no less than a reassessment of the very systems and assumptions which have permitted the mastery of technology over humankind, not only in the West but throughout the human community. The task of the church is to reinterpret the existential threat of the climate catastrophe as a human problem only fully understood in Christ and to communicate this both as an indictment and an opportunity for hope

---

56. Larry Rasmussen, 'Bonhoeffer and the Anthropocene', in *Stellenbosch Theological Journal* 55/Supp 1 (2015): 944–5.

57. Klein, *This Changes Everything*.

58. Susan Abraham, *Identity, Ethics, and Non violence in Post colonial Theory: A Rahnerian Theological Assessment* (New York: Palgrave MacMillan, 2007), 194.

59. Dietrich Bonhoeffer, *Creation and Fall: A Theological Exposition of Genesis 1–3*, edited by John W de Gruchy, translated by Douglas Stephen Bax (Minneapolis: Fortress, 1997), 67.

60. '*Dem Rad selbst in die Speichen zu fallen*,' understood as unhitching a cart from the horse pulling it. Bonhoeffer, *DBWE* 12, 267. Bonhoeffer's use here means 'to bring the apparatus of the unjust and illegitimate state to a halt' and the usual English translation is 'to seize the wheel', see n. 12.

and active response. Bonhoeffer's own seeking of 'who Christ really is for us today' has currency in the contemporary world. The climate crisis, the result of humanity's violence to Earth in a faulty attempt at mastery, can only be addressed as the new humanity enacts *Stellvertretung* and, in doing so, participates in the suffering of Christ and becomes fully human.

The gospel of peace, which so captured Bonhoeffer from around the time of his conversion experience of engaging with the Bible and with the Christ of the Sermon on the Mount, stands in contrast here with the struggles of war and with nature. Both are reassessed under Christ. Bonhoeffer's solution to The Right to Self-Assertion transcends both the Western and Eastern responses and spoke, in his own time, into the pre-war situation. It has contemporary relevance by speaking into the current struggle with nature, and with wars, which together are already yielding up the first waves of victim refugees. A Christian response to the compelling moral problem of climate justice, recently typified in the figure of the lifeless little body of Aylan Kurdi[61] washed ashore, and in many others like it, would see the struggle for the mastery of nature and the mastery of technology together as manifestations of humanity's war against itself. To this end, Bonhoeffer offers both a way of theologically interrogating the problem and a potential way forward to address the planetary crisis.

---

61. Photographed by Nilufer Demir from Turkey's Dogan News Agency and reproduced in many of the world's news papers as well as on social media after 2 Sept 2015, Olivier Laurent, 'What the Image of Alan Kurdi Says About the Power of Photography', Time Inc., at <http://time.com/4022765/aylan-kurdi-photo>. Accessed 30 October 2015.

Some Limits on the Use of Armed Force under the *Sharia*

Asmi Wood

The Prophet said 'One will not enter Paradise whose neighbour is not secure from their wrongful conduct'.[1]

Introduction

This essay examines some legal elements of the use of force under the *sharia* popularly known as an armed *djihad* (armed struggle), including and focusing on actions that may result in environmental damage and harm to non-human sentient beings. While a comprehensive examination of *djihad* is beyond the scope of this essay,[2] there is a gap in the *sharia* literature, on aspects of animal cruelty and ecological effects of war, aspects which are broadly examined here. Armed fighting is permitted under the classical *sharia*,[3] defined generally here as the law derived directly from the primary sources of the *sharia* viz, the

---

1. Abu'l Hussain Muslim, *Al Jami'us Sahih,* vol. 1 (Beirut: Dar al Arabia, 1972), 32.
2. The *sharia* laws of war more broadly are covered extensively in the literature, including in English: Majid Khadduri, *War and Peace in the Law of Islam* (Baltimore: John Hopkins University Press, 1955); Khaled Abou El-Fadl, *Rebellion and Violence in Islamic Law* (Cambridge: Cambridge University Press, 2001); Rudolph Peters, *Crime and Punishment in Islamic Law: Theory and Practice from the Sixteenth to the Twenty-first Century* (Cambridge: Cambridge University Press, 2005).
3. The term classical *sharia* refers here to the accretion of law and jurisprudence over the centuries and is contrasted with a *de novo* contemporary interpretation of the primary texts.

Qur'an and the *hadith* or *sunna* (the traditions of the Prophet).[4] However, the *sharia* holds that Muslims must not initiate hostilities, except tactically in self-defence.[5] The notion of what constitutes self-defence is fairly settled but some contemporary armed Muslim groups have sought greatly to expand the notion, perhaps for the over whelming military strength of their enemies and is of concern in cases, but in any event is an expansion that needs to be closely examined for lawfulness. Once hostilities have commenced however, Muslims must fight without turning back,[6] rightly motivated (Qur'an 9:5).[7] Muslims may slay enemy *combatants* until fighting can lawfully cease but in all cases *must* only use means of fighting that are *intra vires.*

Generally, killing and wanton destruction, even in war, is strenuously to be avoided.[8] The capture of the enemy is preferable, if possible, as it gives the Muslims a chance to invite them to Islam. Further, Muslims are permitted to collect war booty such as arms and livestock, and this encourages the preservation chattels. Further, in the past when slavery was lawful, the captured live person also had an economic value. On the other hand, the spectre of war and slavery were disincentives for Muslims, where historically Muslim slaves were

---

4. Wael B Hallaq, *Law and Legal Theory in Classical and Medieval Islam* (Aldershot: Ashgate, 1994); Wael B Hallaq, *A History of Islamic Legal Theories* (Cambridge: Cambridge University Press, 1997); Wael B Hallaq, *The Origins and Evolution of Islamic Law* (Cambridge: Cambridge University Press, 2005); Nadirsyah Hosen, *Sharia and Constitutional Reform in Indonesia* (Singapore: Institute of Southeast Asian Studies, 2007); Cherif Bassiouni (editor), *The Islamic Criminal Justice System* (Dobbs-Ferry, NY: Oceana, 1982); Cherif Bassiouni and Gamal M Badr, 'The Shariah: Sources, Interpretation, and Rule-Making', *UCLA Journal of Islamic and Near Eastern Law* 1 (2002): 135; Abou El-Fadl, *Rebellion and Violence in Islamic Law*; Peters, *Crime and Punishment in Islamic Law*; Asmi Wood, 'The Position of the Niqab (Face Veil) in Australia under Australian and Islamic Laws', *American Journal of Islamic Social Sciences*, 29/3 (2012): 106, 110.

5. Khadduri, *War and Peace in the Law of Islam*, 59. For example, the Meccan army which had travelled 300 miles to fight the Muslim community in Medina were fought by the Muslims at Badr, a town 80 miles from Medina.

6. According to Muhammad Asad, *The Message of the Qur'an: Translated and Explained* (Gibraltar: Dar al-Andalus,1984), 120. Qur'an 4:84 cannot be an incitement to war, but can only refer to a war in train: 'Then fight in God's cause thou art held responsible only for thyself and rouse the believers. It may be that God will restrain the fury of the unbelievers: for God is the strongest in might and in punishment.'

7. Khadduri, *War and Peace in the Law of Islam*, 60.

8. Qur'an 5:32 among many other verses, some of which are discussed in this essay.

tortured until they gave up their faith or died. On the other hand, the Qur'an prohibits Muslims from torture or forcing people, including their captives, to convert to Islam (Quran 2:256), although proselytisation among captives prior to manumission is strongly encouraged (Quran 41:33). While clearly prohibited, however what actually constitutes 'torture' under the *sharia* is not entirely clear and needs to be clarified for contemporary exigencies, although collecting taxes from *dhimmis* out in the hot sun was described in terms of torture by the Prophet's Companions.[9]

Further, the Muslim soldier is reminded that victory is from God alone and therefore employing foul or *ultra vires* means or wanton killing and destruction, including of animals and plants, things on which other life—all creations of the same God—depends, and must be avoided assiduously, as a satanic 'temptation' (Qur'an 8:48) leading, *at best*, to a short term, illusory, gain, or a pyrrhic victory with a longer term strict punishment for believing Muslims, which is likely, for disobeying or wilfully acting in breach of God's law, (i.e. for breaching the *sharia* prohibitions).[10]

In examining these issues, Part 1 very briefly examines the preconditions necessary for conducting hostilities, including identifying when hostilities can or must cease. Part 2 examines the question of who and what may, and may not, lawfully be targeted during hostilities, with some focus on the environmental effects. Part 3 examines the issue of fighting in 'mixed population' areas (i.e. both military and civilian) and the related collateral damage, injury and death caused to both (non-combatant) humans and other living things. The essay closes with some concluding remarks.

Part 1: Conditions for commencing an armed *djihad*

Muhammad Asad notes, in accordance with the classical *sharia*, that the conditions that make fighting legitimate for Muslims are speci-

---

9. Michael Cook, *Commanding Right and Forbidding Wrong in Islamic Thought* (Cambridge: Cambridge University Press, 2001), 61, quoting the *hadith* of the Prophet that: "Those who torture people in this world will be tortured by God in the next."
10. See above n. 6.

fied in the Qur'an at verses 2:190–195.[11] Once the need and legality, for the use of force has been determined by the legitimate leader, the emphasis then shifts to the lawful means that can be used in this *djihad* and which *must* not be exceeded or breached.

The Qur'an permits Muslims to fight in self-defence,[12] including in collective self-defence.[13] However, according to Majid Khadduri:

> The classical doctrine of *jihad* made no distinction between defensive and offensive war, for in the pursuance of the establishment of God's Sovereignty and Justice on Earth the difference between defensive and offensive acts was irrelevant.[14]

This is not to say that the wars fought by the early Muslims were offensive. To the contrary they were defensive wars. In the early periods of Islam when the Prophet sought sanctuary in Medina, the Meccans sought to destroy the Muslims in Medina (the first Muslim city/state). The two cities are about 300 miles apart.[15] The first major battle fought by Muslims *away* from Medina was the battle for Mecca.[16] This battle was not initiated by the Muslims, but of Muslims responding to treaty obligations

---

11. Asad, *The Message of the Qur'an*, 264. Asad states that the conditions for war are specified in Qur'an 9:12–13 and Qur'an 2:190–95 which read as follows (emphasis added):
    Fight in the cause of God those who fight you but do not transgress limits; for God loveth not transgressors.
    And slay them wherever ye catch them and turn them out from where they have turned you out; for tumult and oppression are worse than slaughter; but fight them not at the Sacred Mosque unless they (first) fight you there; but if they fight you slay them. Such is the reward of those who suppress faith.
    But if they cease, God is Oft-Forgiving Most Merciful.
    And fight them on until there is no more tumult or oppression and there prevail justice and faith in God; but if they cease let there be no hostility except to those who practice oppression.
12. Qur'an 2:190–91 (i.e. those who legitimately may be fought in self-defence (النفسعندفاعً)). The word *qital* قتال is translated as fighting and also means killing.
13. Robert L Phillips, 'Combatancy, Noncombatancy, and Non-combatant Immunity in Just War Tradition', in *Cross, Crescent, and Sword: The Justification and Limitation of War in Western and Islamic Tradition*, edited by James Turner Johnson and John Kelsay (Westport, CT: Greenwood Press, 1990), 197, 200.
14. Khadduri, The Islamic Conception of Justice.
15. See also above n. 4.
16. This historical event is often referred to as *fathmakkah* (or the opening of Mecca).

under a pact of mutual defence.[17] The Muslims and their allies were victorious. The magnanimous treatment subsequently afforded by the Prophet to the vanquished Meccans,[18] many of whom had been guilty of serious crimes against the then minority Meccan Muslim community, indicates that even in the face of the most egregious and dire conditions, that looting, pillage, revenge or retribution were not, and arguably therefore, should never be, a motive for or the result of, an armed *djihad*.[19]

On the contrary, Muslims must sue for peace whenever possible,[20] not only in their capacity as individuals, but also collectively as groups, arguably in contemporary language, including States as well as non-state actors. The Qur'anic obligation is on every Muslim to avoid war, including wars conducted on 'righteous' pretexts, when the 'real aim' is greed, or in Qur'anic parlance, for 'worldly gain' (Qur'an 4:94).[21]

Rudolph Peters notes that despite some verses that allow the Muslims 'to fight the unbelievers unconditionally …Classical Muslim Koran interpretation, however, did not go into this direction.'[22] This is the better interpretation of the permission to fight, one that has now crystallised into an Islamic customary norm. Contemporary Muslims, sometimes seeking territory or resources, but sometimes also fighting severely oppressive regimes, have attempted instrumentally to reverse or at least modify these established *sharia* norms. Essentially they have done so by subscribing to, and in many cases even in breach of, the more permissive international norms, often simul-

---

17. Adil Salahi, *Muhammad: Man and Prophet* (Mark field: Islamic Foundation, 2002), 608; Martin Lings, *Mecca from before Genesis until Now* (Cambridge, UK: Archetype, 2004), 25.

18. Lings, Mecca from before Genesis until Now, 26.

19. The record of armed conflicts after the death of the Prophet and his early companions, seems to make the defensive nature of contemporary Muslims' wars much more ambiguous. While there are some not able exceptions, as the Muslim community are chronologically further removed from the time of the Prophet, their record with respect to their rulers engaging in purely defensive wars becomes less clear. Later Muslims become more like their own contemporaries with respect to the use of war in settling disputes and acquiring territory and power, although they used the epithet of *djihad* arguably to give the ruler greater credibility among ordinary Muslims.

20. See below n. 42.

21. Farhad Malekian, The Concept of Islamic International Criminal Law: A Comparative Study (Dordrecht: Springer, 1994), 50.

22. Rudolph Peters, *Jihad in Classical and Modern Islam: A Reader* (Princeton: Markus Wiener, 1996), 2.

taneously while claiming to be engaged in *djihad*, claims that should therefore be carefully examined by jurists. Note that the *sharia* has a rebuttable presumption of continuity of laws and is similar to the common law doctrine of precedent.[23] Many contemporary Islamic fighters appear to refuse to concede that they are bound by precedent but on the other hand behave as if they free to re-examine questions of *djihad de novo,* often instrumentally. These contemporary fighters are aided by an international community that rejects the *sharia* out of hand and Muslims who appears to be too timid to call to account Muslim warmongers of every ilk or alternatively claim that this 'silence' is not intentional but it is because they are too weak to be heard.

Note that Qur'anic permission to fight, including in self-defence or against oppression, does not necessarily require aggression to have a nexus to a State, as is the case under contemporary international law.[24] The *sharia* does not provide States a monopoly on the use of force,[25] nor is it interpreted as such by custom.[26] On the other hand,

---

23. Wael B Hallaq, 'Was the Gate of Ijtihad Closed?', International Journal of Middle Eastern Studies 16/1 (1984): 3–41; Muneer Goolan Fareed, *Legal Reform in the Muslim World: The Anatomy of a Scholarly Dispute in the 19th and Early 20th Centuries on the Usage of Ijtihad as a Legal Tool* (San Francisco: Austin & Winfield, 1996).

24. While self-defence is recognised under international law, for space and context this body of law will not be considered here, particularly because none of al-Qa'eda's wrongs cites colonialism as a relevant factor.

25. As a legal issue however, ascertaining the existence of an armed conflict (including border protection), is a question of law fact. Self-defence is permitted under the UN Charter (Article 51); in general international law: RY Jennings, 'The Caroline and McLeod Cases' *American Journal of International Law,* 32/1 (1938): 82; *Case concerning the Military and Paramilitary Activities in and against Nicaragua (Nicaragua v United States of America), Merits, (Judgment of 27 June 1986)* 14 ICJ Rep 1, 14, see <http://www.icj-cij.org/docket/?sum=367&p1=3& p2=3&case=70&p3=5>. Accessed 27 November 2016; as well as in Islamic law (Qur'an 2:190). While Article 51 is silent as to the 'source of the aggression', it is not limited to aggression emanating from a Member State: DW Greig, 'Invalidity and the Law of Treaties', *British Institute of International and Comparative Law Occasional Paper Number Seven* (2006), 110. The Qur'anic 'right' of self-defence is not limited to a 'Member of the United Nations' and is enjoyed by all injured or oppressed groups.

26. There is a Qur'anic injunction that Muslims should obey their leaders but this verse puts obedience to God and the Prophet first (Qur'an 4:59). In practice this means that leaders should only be obeyed as long as they do not disobey God and the Prophet, *ipso facto* making the leaders 'disobedient' if they do oppress their subjects.

all contemporary Muslim States (defined here as nation states with a Muslim majority) are members of the UN. These States are secular and operate in accordance with the international norm which gives states a monopoly on the use of violence. Some Muslim states have *inter alia* used state sovereignty as a legal basis to clamp down hard on internal dissent, at times resulting in internal resistance that is often framed around Islamic language, including calls for armed *djihad*.[27]

In summary, the *sharia's* interpretation on the scope of armed self-defence, which extends to individuals and groups, arguably is therefore broader than international law. This, it can be argued, is problematic under contemporary international law which grants States the right to sovereignty and, with some minimal oversight on human rights issues, results in a right to manage their domestic affairs free of foreign intervention. This divergence on views on the scope of the rights and obligations of rulers and individuals within a nation state, as opposed to the more individualistic rights and obligations framework of Islam,[28] which permits Muslims to oppose these oppressive rulers, can lead to a confusion when solely viewed under international norms.

Permitted aims means of armed djihad

The proper purpose of war generally, and of the means employed in its conduct, *always* is to achieve a lawful objective. To be legitimate, armed *djihad* must inter alia be conducted for the prescribed limited *sharia* purposes and aims. In addition to the spiritual aims of *djihad* (only incidentally examined here), the two main practical aims of armed *djihad* are (i) to create (capacity that provides) deterrence against attack and (ii) the capacity to subdue the enemy.[29]

---

27. While not discussed here, a contemporary example is the States' clampdown on dissent in the after math of the so called 'Arab Spring' including the current unrest in Egypt, Syria and Libya.
28. See below discussions at nn. 78 and 79.
29. The question of who constitutes the 'enemy' is a key question and a shorthand term for those whom Muslims might be permitted to fight under the *sharia*.

The permitted reasons do not include fighting for hatred, resources or revenge.[30] All life is sacred, often read down as referring to human life, and taking life except for lawful reasons, is a serious, punishable crime (Qur'an 5:32).[31]

The Qur'an provides the principles and some guidance on these 'means', related prohibitions, as well as some important *exceptions* for necessity that may be used in armed *djihad* (Qur'an 61:10–13)[32] The Qur'an and *sunna* urge Muslims to be trust worthy and to act honourably and honestly; this is clearly the spirit in which legal principles surrounding both the use of weapons and their necessary exceptions must be examined (Qur'an 2:173).[33] Consequently, unlawful 'means' shall not be used or carved out instrumentally as exceptions as a pre text to justify 'the ends'. Simply stated, the objectives of an armed *djihad* must be lawful, the means used in achieving these objectives must be lawful and every command that goes to both the means used and achieving of each objective of an armed *djihad* must also *all* be lawful.

Some explicitly prohibited 'means of warfare' include, intentionally killing by fire or other means that cause prolonged suffering to sentient beings.[34] Further, humiliating or dis honouring the dignity of a human person, sexual misconduct (Qur'an 4:15;Qur'an 24:4) or further depriving ordinary people and animals of food or water, are all prohibited under the *sharia*. These *sharia* limits are often not

---

30. Qur'an 5:8: 'O ye who believe! stand out firmly for God as witnesses to fair dealing and let not the hatred of others to you make you swerve to wrong and depart from justice. Be just: that is next to Piety: and fear God for God is well-acquainted with all that ye do.' Convicted JI operatives knew that 'revenge' is not a permitted reason for armed *djihad*: Di Martin, 'Tackling Indonesian Terror', in Background Briefing ABC, 23 September 2007. For a discussion of 'war' under international law, see Yoram Dinstein, *War, Aggression, and Self-defence* (4th ed., Cambridge: Cambridge University Press, 2005), 3.

31. Further, the Qur'an categorises the unjust taking of a single life, with no further qualification, as equivalent to the slaying of all of humanity.

32. Khadduri, *The Islamic Conception of Justice*, 168.

33. That is, one who honestly acts out of necessity but 'without wilful disobedience nor transgressing due limits (is guiltless)'.

34. Muhammad Al-Mughirah al-Bukhari, *The Translations of the Meaning of Sahih al-Bukhari*, vol. 1 (Chicago: Kazi Publications, 1976), 398.; Muhammad Al-Mughirah al-Bukhari, *The Translations of the Meaning of Sahih al-Bukhari*, vol. 3 (Chicago: Kazi Publications, 1976), 323.

honoured by contemporary Muslim fighters perhaps for practicality but sometimes also for instrumental reasons. Nonetheless, this essay takes a normative approach seeking to identify the broadly applicable law, while conceding that there are some exceptions not comprehensively identified or discussed.

Proselytising by force is also prohibited (Qur'an 2:256). In Islam, 'guidance' is God's *sole* prerogative (Qur'an 24:46; Qur'an 35:8) and consequently Muslim hegemony is not a pre-requisite either for guidance or for that matter the practice of Islam, which can be done in secret, particularly during oppressive times.[35] The *only* desirable state for the practice of the faith is that one has *freely* chosen to do so, and is able to do so to the best of one's ability. However, Muslims as the inheritors of the Prophet do have a pastoral duty to invite people to the Muslim faith (Qur'an 16:125), thus giving every human being the opportunity to hear[36] and then freely to accept or reject the Prophet's message, so that then they alone will be responsible for their choices (Quran 2:256). Therefore, armed '*djihad*' for the propagation of the faith, for the subjugation of peoples or for socio-economic reasons (such as for marriage, but nonetheless practiced by Muslims), have no intrinsic Islamic value[37] either for the *djihadist*[38] or the 'newly force converted Muslim' because faith not sincerely and voluntarily accepted is no faith (Qur'an 2:256; Qur'an 109:6).[39] On the other hand, 'belief' or 'conversion' by or of non-Muslims for instrumental or 'worldly' reasons has little religious value, as is *djihad* that is fought other than in self-defence or for preventing persecution. In Islam, hypocrisy (a *sharia* crime, but one that is only punished in

---

35. That is, Muslims have survived and prospered both as majorities as well as minorities.

36. Qur'an 9:6: 'If one amongst the pagans ask thee for asylum grant it to him so that he may hear the word of God and then escort him to where he can be secure: that is because they are men without knowledge.'

37. According to al-Bukhari, *The Translations of the Meaning of Sahih al-Bukhari,* vol. 3, 424. the Prophet said: 'The (reward of) deeds depend on intentions, and every person will get the reward according to intent …'

38. The reason is that 'forced conversion' involves breaching an explicit command of the Qur'an that there is to be no compulsion in faith (Qur'an 2:256).

39. However, since repentance is always possible, and the person 'repents hypocrisy' and then freely accepts 'genuine faith' sometime before his/her death.

the Hereafter) is worse than disbelief (Qur'an 2:6; Qur'an 2:9)[40] and those who 'accept' faith for material reasons or for reasons other than as a commitment to submit to God alone, are forewarned of the dire consequences of this 'treachery' against themselves (Qur'an 4:145). Thus, wars for the purpose of conversion or subjugation, the pursuit of land, wealth or resources, or the destruction of nature and its living things are all arguably anti-ethical in the meaning of the *sharia*. However, the practical benefit for the rulers in a larger population, taxation base or resource availability, are clearly relevant factors but which do not find a legal basis under the *sharia*.

Part 2: Conditions for ceasing an armed *djihad*.

Generally, an armed conflict ceases when one party is defeated or surrenders, the parties agree mutually to cease hostilities or perhaps through the exhaustion of the parties to the conflict. These are practical criteria. The Qur'anic criteria are that fighting should continue (if lawful and practical to do so) 'until there is no more persecution' and 'the enemy is subdued' (Qur'an 2:193).[41] The Quranic 'peace verse' on the other hand obliges Muslims to respond to overtures of peace.[42] While Muslims must be aware that an offer of peace might be a ruse, they should nonetheless proceed with trust in God alone.[43] Where practical, the terms of peace that are negotiated by or for Muslims must be fair, just for all parties and, whenever possible, ensure that the conditions of aggression or oppression that had triggered the fighting, in the first instance, will have ceased.

---

40. Moreover, punishment for disbelief *kufr* is described as 'awesome' (Qur'an 2:6), as compared with 'grievous' for hypocrisy *nifaq* (نفاق) (Qur'an 2:9). Further, the Qur'an states that *'almunafiqeena fi darkilasfali min an nar'* (the hypocrites will be in the deepest point in hell) (Qur'an 4:145). This position on hypocrisy is not dissimilar to the biblical view in which hypocrites 'will receive a more severe judgment', John Carroll, *The Existential Jesus* (Carlton North: Scribe, 2007), 90.
41. Ahmad Hasan, *The Early Development of Islamic Jurisprudence* (Islamabad: Islamic Research Institute, 1970), 8.
42. Qur'an 8:61: 'But if the enemy incline towards peace do thou (also) incline towards peace ...' On the other hand, there is a view shared by some that this 'peace verse' was abrogated: Peters, *Jihad in Classical and Modern Islam*, 39.
43. Qur'an 8:62 (emphasis added): '*Should they intend to deceive thee verily God sufficeth thee*: He it is that hath strengthened thee with his aid and with (the company of) the believers.'

Part 3: Identifying legitimate/illegitimate targeting of people

The *sharia* prohibits the killing of some and permits the lawful killing of others during armed *djihad*. Such groups are identified and will be examined below. The question related to the development of the contemporary law relates principally to persons who may not fall within one of these two explicit categories in present day communities. The presumption during legitimate armed combat must be that if the taking of life of a member of a particular group or class is explicitly permitted under the *sharia*, then this is lawful. Section 2 identifies the Qur'anic classes of people (combatants) who may be fought and, by clear implication, may be targeted and killed when necessary, although, as mentioned, capture is preferable.[44] However, if the *sharia* explicitly prohibits or is silent on a group or class ('protected persons' discussed in Section 1 below), then it must *remain unlawful* to do so, unless in the latter case, some exception such as *sharia* 'necessity' is identified by the jurists. There is however a grey area between these two explicit classes that must be re-examined by jurists of every age. Further, it is not settled, or at least unclear, whether 'military necessity' under international law also qualifies as *sharia* 'necessity'. The notion of mutual recognition between these two systems, while clearly important, is a broad topic for discussion and is not explicitly explored here.

Unlike under international humanitarian law (IHL), the permissibility of attacks which will *certainly* result in collateral deaths during targeting is not settled under the *sharia*. While not discussed here, accidental killing under the *sharia* (as distinct from intentional collateral killing) draws compensation to the families of the victims.[45]

Section 1: Protected persons who may not intentionally be killed

Islam categorises the unjust taking of a single (human) life, with no further qualification, as the slaying of all humanity (Qur'an 5:32). Further, even in an armed *djihad*, which forms a general exception to the taking of life, the Prophet forbade slaying 'hermits … the old and

----

44. See below n. 70.
45. Khaleed Abou El Fadl, 'The Rules of Killing at War: An Inquiry into Classical Sources', *The Muslim World*, LXXXIX (1999): 144–56, 144.

the decrepit, children or women'[46] and ordered Muslims 'not to break promises, not to kill a child, a woman, an old man or monk praying in seclusion.'[47] The prohibitions of the orthodox caliphs, discussed below, are also considered binding by the vast majority of Muslims. The first orthodox caliph Abu Bakr commanded:

> Do not kill old men, women or minors, at the time of encounter of the armies, *in the heat of the battle* or at the time of an expected attack. *Do not cut date palms; do not kill animals except for food*, leave people in convents and seclusion alone. Do not kill *sick people* or monks. Do not commit treachery, cheat, mutilate or show cowardice …[48]

The second orthodox caliph, Omar I, issued the following command to his armies:

> Do not kill old men, women or minors, at the time of encounter of the armies, in *the heat of the battle* or at the time of an expected attack.[49]

The fourth orthodox caliph, Ali bin Abu Talib did not prosecute a rebellious armed group known as the *khawarij* even though they vociferously and violently opposed his rule.[50] It was only when the *khawarij* killed the governor and they refused to surrender the killer, that Ali fought them as a group.[51] For the orthodox caliphs, opposition or dissent were not ground for an armed response. Note also that in theory under *Shi'i* Islam all opponents of the legitimate imam may be fought.[52] For the 'absence' (occultation) however of the rightful

---

46. Peters, *Jihad in Classical and Modern Islam*, 49.
47. Salahi, *Muhammad*, 596. There are several similar *hadith* with slight variations not cited here.
48. Muhammad Hamidullah, *Muslim Conduct of State* (3rd ed., Lahore: Muhammad Ashraf, 1953), 314 (emphasis added).
49. Hamidullah, *Muslim Conduct of State*, 315 (emphasis added).
50. Abou El-Fadl, *Rebellion and Violence in Islamic Law*, 34.
51. Abou El-Fadl, *Rebellion and Violence in Islamic Law*, 152.
52. Sohail H Hashmi, 'Islamic Ethics and Weapons of Mass Destruction: An Argument for Non-proliferation' in *Ethics and Weapons of Mass Destruction: Religious and Secular Perspectives*, edited by Sohail H Hashmi and Steven P Lee (Cambridge: Cambridge University Press, 2004), 321, 325.

Shi'i imam, differences with *Sunni* Islam are not relevant in practice.[53] Further, although Omar II, an Umayyad, was not an orthodox caliph, many Muslims consider his precedent as authoritative.[54] Omar II ordered his troops not to kill women or children, execute prisoners,[55] pursue a fugitive or kill the wounded and based these decisions on the Qur'an.[56] There is also consensus further, that the protected categories include visitors (*must'amin*),[57] Scriptuaries (people following the religions of previous prophets such as Jews and Christians) and persons covered by treaty (Qur'an 2:177). Generally the killing of women, old men, priests and nuns or children, provided that they are not fighters,[58] is prohibited under the *sharia*.[59]

It is noted here for convenience and for future reference that these classical prohibitions can be abstracted as a *general principle against killing those unable or at least unlikely to fight against Muslims* and also prohibiting the wanton or unnecessary destruction of the environment and enemy property.

On the other hand, Sohail Hashimi points out that *hadith* such as those of the orthodox caliphs referred to above must be interpreted as: 'it is the [enemy's] *capacity to fight*, not belief or rejection of Islam, that is the criterion for determining liability to damage in war', and goes on to state that these prohibitions do not find equivalence with

---

53. HAR Gibb and JH Kramers (editors), *Concise Encyclopaedia of Islam* (4th ed, Leiden: Brill, 2001), 110.
54. Muhammad Baqir As-Sadr, *Lessons in Islamic Jurisprudence* (Oxford: One world, 2005), 6.
55. The many *hadith* that relate to this point on POWs provides a strong legal basis in principle for the validity in principle of GCIII under the *sharia*. Specific provisions however, need to be individually examined for legal validity.
56. Abou El-Fadl, *Rebellion and Violence in Islamic Law*, 37 esp. n 21, referring to Qur'an 2:190.
57. *Must'amin* are people granted temporary access to Muslim lands for trade, pilgrimage or transit and are protected. The word *must'amin* literally means 'one granted security', Milton J Cowan (editor), *The Hans Wehr Dictionary of Modern Written Arabic* (Beirut: Librairie du Liban, 1980), 28.
58. Peters, *Jihad in Classical and Modern Islam*, 33; Salahi, *Muhammad*, 475. The *sharia* was developed later after the Prophet when Muslims encountered priests that did fight (for example such as Burmese priests in the present day Burma).
59. Muhammad Al-Mughirah al-Bukhari, *The Translations of the Meaning of Sahih al-Bukhari*, vol 4 (Chicago: Kazi Publications, 1976), 158; Abu'l Hussain Muslim, *Al Jami'usSahih*, vol 3 (Beirut: Dar al Arabia, 1972), 946; Peters, *Jihad in Classical and Modern Islam*, 13, 172 n. 6.

the contemporary concept of non-combatant immunity.[60] Peters' view, although not identical, is similar to that of Hashimi and states that all able bodied enemy may be killed.[61]

However, Hashmi's and Peters' views appear quite broad in their scope and should not be considered the position on which there is Muslim consensus. For example, the *hadith* holds, when there is no open conflict, that able-bodied hypocrites (often living among Muslims, claimed to be Muslims yet agitated and fought against Muslims), may not be killed, even if they are armed, although they clearly possess a capacity (and more importantly even a clear and open desire to defeat Islam). Further, while old men and minors (whose killing is prohibited by the Prophet and the orthodox caliphs) prima facie may not have the capacity to fight, some hermits, women, the sick and wounded may possess a capacity to fight.

Therefore, it is proposed that a form of words that may serve as a *starting* position to reflect the contemporary *sharia* position is:

> There is a rebuttable presumption that all people who are not directly involved in fighting against Muslims (and their allies, as discussed in section 2 below), engaged in lawful armed conflict, may not be killed. Conversely, that those who are fighting against Muslims (and their allies) may be killed, if necessary, but that capture is preferable especially if they are *not* Muslims.[62] Animals should not be killed or plants damaged except for food.

It is suggested that this is a form of words, *prima facie*, that fits in with the spirit of the classical position on targeting during lawful combat. People are invited to critique this position so that some consensus might evolve and perhaps crystallise. This is perhaps a possible antidote to the permissiveness of the 'means of war' present in contemporary armed conflicts *inter alia* involving Muslims.

---

60. Hashmi, 'Islamic Ethics and Weapons of Mass Destruction', 321, 326 (emphasis added).

61. See below text accompanying n. 64.

62. While this issue is not fully settled and not examined in detail, it is noted that Muslim rebels who die in conflict are said to have receive their punishment here and therefore not punished for this rebellion any further in the Hereafter. Non-Muslim captives however, may be afforded the opportunity to hear the message of the Prophet.

Section 2: Who and what may legitimately be targeted in armed djihad?

The Qur'an permits fighting, and if necessary includes permission to kill those who fight Muslims (Qur'an 2:190),[63] those who drive Muslims out of their homes (Qur'an 2:191), those who oppress (Qur'an 2:191), or in some circumstances, those who cause *fitna* (broadly translated here as sedition), which is accompanied by armed fighting. However, the notion of '*fitna*' has instrumentally been used by modern states a basis/pretext for supressing opposition to oppressive rule. Properly characterised however, 'fighting *fitna*' arguably fits within self-defence. Within these limits, all adult able-bodied enemy males (although while not settled under the *sharia*, can reasonably be extended to fighting females),[64] including polytheists (Qur'an 9:5)[65] may be slain or taken prisoner (Qur'an 47:4),[66] and is a position not dissimilar to that under contemporary international law related to armed conflict.

---

63. Muslims did not engage in fighting even under and during oppression in Mecca. The Christian perspective that fighting was prohibited, and in the absence of its explicit abrogation through the Qur'an at that time, was probably considered binding on Muslims as under Isa 2:4: 'Nation shall not lift up sword against nation; neither shall they learn war anymore.' It was only after the revelation of Qur'an 22:39 (in Medina) that Muslims engaged in self-defence (and who until then had legal grounds to believe that the law on the prohibition on war was still in force).

64. Peters, *Jihad in Classical and Modern Islam*, 33. The scope of Qur'an 47:4 is similar to the IHL provision that deems all members of the armed forces as combatants, Jean-Marie Henckaerts and Louise Doswald-Beck (editors), *Customary International Humanitarian Law, vol. I* (Cambridge: Cambridge University Press, 2005), 4.

65. Asad, *The Message of the Qur'an*, 256 n. 8. There is a further condition that treaty arrangements between the parties are absent, suspended or revoked.

66. Unless the individual was invited to Islam (and has declined), then capture is preferable because the person concerned will then be in a position in which to hear the call to, be offered the opportunity to learn and then accept or reject the Muslim Covenant. Often a promise by the prisoner that s/he will study the Covenant is all that is required to discharge the Muslim's duty to *da'wa* (call to the faith) (Qur'an 3:20). See the promise to study Islam extracted by the Taliban from Yvonne Ridley as a condition for her release, Yvonne Ridley, *In the Hands of the Taliban* (London: Robson Books, 2001), 209. In former times when slavery was a legal institution, Muslims had the additional economic incentive to capture rather than kill an opponent for the potential economic value of the unhurt slave in good health.

On the specific question of *fitna* mentioned above, the Qur'an states that when two parties of Muslims are in conflict, if the party that has transgressed 'beyond bounds'[67] should be fought by all other Muslims,[68] creating an exception to the prohibition against the slaying of Muslims (Qur'an 2:193; Qur'an 8:39),[69] and also forms a legal basis for fighting oppression when perpetrated by the rulers or even non-state actors such as ISIS.

Generally however, the capture of the enemy is preferable to killing.[70] A person who is no longer a threat or who seeks asylum must, as far as practical, be given asylum/sanctuary, *inter alia* so that he or she may hear the message of the Prophet (Qur'an 9:6).[71] Those who are *hors de combat* but accompanying the army may also be captured, and in the past wives and children of soldiers (who during wars in the pre-Islamic times in Arabia usually accompanied the men to war) and consequently were taken captive when a war was lost. This war was a clear deterrent to aggressive wars, but the fuller discussion of this aspect of war is outside the scope of this essay.

Captives may be ransomed, used in prisoner exchange programmes or used to bring literacy or other skills to the Muslim community. Through skills transfer captives may earn their freedom,[72] a concept arguably not known to contemporary IHL. Prisoners of war of limited means may be conditionally released without ransom, for example on their own undertaking that they will not fight against the

---

67. This is a particular translation from the original Arabic.
68. Qur'an 49:9: 'If two parties among the Believers fall into a quarrel make ye peace between them: but if one of them transgresses beyond bounds against the other then fight ye (all) against the one that transgresses until it complies with the command of God; but if it complies then make peace between them with justice and be fair: for God loves those who are fair (and just).' The phrase (المؤمنين من ئفتان طآو إن)—two parties among the Believers—refers to the '2 groups' in the Arabic dual construct, a very specific form that does not envision a set of warring tribes. The verse also uses the word 'believers' as opposed to 'Muslims'.
69. Some exceptions to this rule include the permission to fight (and kill) Muslims 'who transgress beyond bounds against other Muslims' (Qur'an 49:9), and for the execution of *quisas* and *hudud* punishments.
70. Qur'an 9:6: 'If one amongst the pagans ask thee for asylum grant it to him so that he may hear the word of God and then escort him to where he can be secure: that is because they are men without knowledge.'
71. See above n.66, and below n. 73, on the contemporary example of Yvonne Ridley POW.
72. Salahi, *Muhammad*, 283.

Muslims in future or under took to study Islam.[73] This is arguably an area of law in which the *sharia* can make a contribution to IHL, and while outside the scope of this essay, is an issue that should be examined in some detail.

Further, the Qur'an also enumerates, some groups of those who may be fought. These groups are now considered. Self-evident categories are simply named. These categories are:

1. 'Those who fight Muslims': The right to self-defence is universally accepted at law under most if not all legal systems.

2. *Ribat* (border protection): *Ribat* (رباط)[74] is the safe guarding of the frontiers of *dār al-Islam* (territory under Islam/Muslims). *Ribat* is lawful, including by the use of force if necessary, and constitutes a special category of collective self-defence.[75] The territorial integrity, political independence and the right of a State to protect its own borders is settled under international law.[76]

3. 'Those who violate their peace treaties': On its face, this ground for war appears to be quite wide. However, as under international law, the *sharia* too would be interpreted quite narrowly so that only a serious violation will trigger a right to self-defence. Further other remedies, not involving the use of force, must be actively considered before fighting is permitted. The *sharia* authority for this category is from the Qur'an (Qur'an 9:12).

---

73. Salahi, *Muhammad*, 283. Although Ridley does not fall into the category of a poor POW, the Taliban nonetheless released her on her own undertaking that she would study the faith. Ridley had tried to obtain a visa for Afghanistan but failing that she had entered Afghanistan clandestinely in circumstances that were not characterised as innocent passage by the Taliban. Ridley, *In the Hands of the Taliban*, 62, 91, 209.

74. Qur'an 8:59–61: 'Let not the unbelievers think that they can get the better (of God): they will never frustrate (them). Against them make ready your strength to the utmost of your power including steeds of war (*ribat al-khayl*) to strike terror into (the hearts of) the enemies of God and your enemies and others besides whom ye may not know but whom God doth know. Whatever ye shall spend in the cause of God shall be repaid unto you and ye shall not be treated unjustly. But if the enemy incline towards peace do thou (also) incline towards peace and trust in God: for He is the one that hears and knows (all things).'

75. Khadduri, *War and Peace in the Law of Islam*, 81. See UN Charter Article 51 for the contemporary international legal position.

76. Article 2 (4) of the UN Charter.

4. 'Those who expel people from their homes': This category or head of power, legitimising armed *djihad*, is also a form of self-defence but is separately and explicitly permitted in the Qur'an (Qur'an 2:191), whether or not the expelled persons or the people guilty of expelling persons are Muslim or otherwise. The Qur'anic test (Qur'an 2:191) is arguably stricter than the international norm against expelling people from their 'land' or 'country'.[77] This category would include people normally classified as 'internally displaced persons (IDPs)' under contemporary international law. Violators may be fought (Qur'an 2:193; Qur'an 8:39). The underlying *sharia* 'right', however, is for the protection of religious freedom (Qur'an 22:40) and arguably is not property rights, protected separately, and not discussed here.

5. 'Those who oppress': The Qur'an obliges Muslims to assist the weak and persecuted (Muslim or otherwise).[78] The Prophet commanded Muslims to oppose oppression every where, including oppression *by* Muslims.[79] The specific meaning of 'oppression' has not been judicially examined in the contemporary Islamic or international

---

77. See discussion on border protection (*ribat*) above.

78. Qur'an 4:75: 'And why should ye not fight in the cause of God and of those who being weak are ill-treated (and oppressed)? Men, women and children whose cry is: "Our Lord! Rescue us from this town whose people are oppressors; and raise for us from Thee one who will protect; and raise for us from Thee one who will help!"' The term used is: (assist the) weak *mustadh'afeen* المستضعفين and not only the 'oppressed'. This is because if the Muslims are not weak they should have their own means of responding and/or moving away from oppression. A case in point is the current liberation of Christian and Yazidi villages in Iraq by the Iraqi Army (which is predominantly *Shi'ite* Muslims) from ISIS control (who are also Muslims), Hollie McKay, 'As Battle to Liberate Mosul Plays out, Yazidis Hope for Healing', Fox News: World (26 October 2016); <http://www.foxnews.com/world/2016/10/19/as-battle-to-liberate-mosul-plays-out-yazidis-hope-for-healing.html>. Accessed 27 November 2016.

79. This idea that Muslims are required to oppose oppression irrespective of the religious affiliation of either the oppressor or oppressed is deeply ingrained in the general Muslim community, even among 'ordinary people'; see, for example, Mamdouh Habib (with Julia Collingwood), *My Story: The Tale of a Terrorist Who Wasn't* (Carlton North: Scribe, 2008), 31. al-Bukhari, *The Translations of the Meaning of Sahih al-Bukhari*, vol 4, 70, narrates: 'The Prophet said, "Help your brother whether he is an oppressor or an oppressed." A man said, "O Prophet! I will help him if he is oppressed, but if he is an oppressor, how shall I help him?" The Prophet said, "By preventing him from oppressing (others), for that is how to help him."'

law contexts and this chapter therefore uses the word in its ordinary contemporary meaning.

6. 'Those who suppress faith': Those who suppress (in practice the Muslim faith, although this is not the plain and ordinary meaning of the provision, Qur'an 2:193; Qur'an 8:39) may, subject to pre-conditions now discussed, also be fought (Qur'an 2:191).[80] Most jurists agree that there is binding obligation on each Muslim to defend the Muslim faith when attacked,[81] even if the imam's authorisation is absent. While defence can take many forms, they must all be intra vires.

7. Hypocrites: As discussed above, the sanctions refer to social sanctions unless they take up arms against the Muslims.

8. 'Leaders of unbelief': Muslims are also instructed to fight the *leaders* of unbelief (Qur'an 9:29), when they violate their peace treaties (see above) *and* taunt Muslims (Qur'an 9:12–13).

9. The 'friends of Satan': The Qur'an permits Muslims to fight 'the friends of Satan' (Qur'an 4:76). This is a broad permissive ground, and one that can be potentially misused unless carefully circumscribed by law. As a general and permissive command it appears to cover actions conducted both during peace and at times of war.

Generally, 'Satan's friends' are described as those who are treacherous and given to 'bad acts' (Qur'an 25:28–29),[82] which must be countered when *manifest* and are discussed below (i.e. taking action against acts that do not affect others remains *ultra vires*, Qur'an 109:6). Muslims, however, are required to 'fight' or combat evil (and in this context not necessarily through the use of force) with what is good (Qur'an 13:22; Qur'an 28:51). The command is *not* one to fight an individual 'bad

---

80. The reason for this interpolation is that the Qur'an states that 'faith' in God's eye is Islam (Qur'an 5:3), but Islam in its broader sense also means 'submission to God's will' (and covers the faith of believing Scriptuaries (e.g. Jews and Christians) (Qur'an 2:62). The former interpretation, however, is less ambiguous.

81. Khadduri, *War and Peace in the Law of Islam*, 95. It is unclear in the circumstances what 'attack' means but it must mean a physical attack because otherwise any criticism of Islam can be deemed an attack. This is not the precedent of the Prophet who, when Islam was verbally attacked, responded with patient exposition and almost always gentle rebuttal. This precedent can be set up in contrast with some contemporary Muslims reacting violently to criticisms (sometimes vile and unwarranted criticisms but verbal criticisms nonetheless) against Islam.

82. Abdullah Yusuf Ali, *The Holy Qur'an: Translation and Commentary* (1980), 932.

person' as subjectively characterised by their opponents but actions that lead to systemic oppression. However, in essence, 'the friends of Satan' are souls given to 'diseases of the heart', most of which, but not all (as mentioned below), are 'diseases' not generally visible to humans and thus only punished in the Hereafter, (i.e. matters outside the jurisdiction of a temporal judge).

In a temporal context, some of these satanic acts, described in the primary sources, are manifest acts which can be opposed and overcome. The means that may be employed against this group are not specifically prescribed and must therefore fall within the general rules circumscribing *djihad*. Clearly, the lawful 'means' should be *intra vires* and clearly are not unlimited.

'Friends of Satan' are variously described as people with certain negative characteristics, including those involved in 'cruel practices' such as slitting the ears of (live) animals (Qur'an 4:119).[83] The more general prohibition on animal cruelty is further developed in another *hadith* of the Prophet that relates the example of a person who had practiced their externally observable elements of the Muslim Covenant (such as prayer, fasting and charitable giving), but was punished in Hell because the family cat was not fed at home and was also locked up inside, thus preventing the cat from foraging for herself.[84] Further, the Prophet [who discouraged the practice of 'cursing' except in extreme injustice] nonetheless *cursed* the one who cut the limb (or some other part) of an animal while it was still alive,[85] which for Muslims effectively constitutes a prohibition and should therefore be prohibited under the positive law.

However, it should be noted that one would 'fight' systemic cruelty as perpetrated by say governments or industry quite differently than one would with an individual pet owner, farmer or others. Prima facie it would appear that Muslims are permitted to 'fight' perpetra-

---

83. In this regards, see 'Pig Identification for on Farm Management', Queensland Government Department of Agriculture and Fisheries, <http://www.daf.qld. gov.au/animal-industries/pigs/managing-a-piggery/identification-on-farm>. Accessed 27 November 2016. With respect to the practice of slitting lambs' ears, see: 'Fur, Leather, and Wool', Save the World, <http://www.youcouldsavetheworld. com/fur_leather_wool.html>. Accessed 27 November 2016.

84. Abu'l Hussain Muslim, *Al Jami'us Sahih*, vol. 4 (Beirut: Dar al Arabia, 1972), 1381.

85. Muhammad Al-Mughirah al-Bukhari, *The Translations of the Meaning of Sahih al-Bukhari*, vol 7 (Chicago: Kazi Publications, 1976), 307.

tors of such animal cruelty such as slitting animal ears, or cutting off the limbs of animals that are still alive, but perhaps through lawful means. This could include advocacy, litigation, demonstrations or economic boycotts of such products, arguably, by encouraging them to desist from such cruel or satanic practices and from desecrating nature (Qur'an 4:119). However, it should not in this instance simply be a gratuitous pretext to support armed action against farmers or others even if they perpetrate such cruel acts.[86]

Not with standing that, while this example is relevant to animal welfare, some of these tortuous practices and worse are equally applied to human beings both during peace times and during war often as a legal ground (say by the U.S. military at Guantanamo and other 'dark sites' where such techniques are euphemistically called 'enhanced interrogation techniques') used for obtaining information, and, as set out by human rights organisations. Regimes which are directly or indirectly responsible for such practices against humans could therefore justifiably also be categorised as 'friends of Satan' and appropriate, and where necessary forceful, action taken. However, and while not equating the moral agency of all species as being equal, there are commonalities in all sentient species. Such commonalities must oblige human beings to exercise ethical and non-cruel behaviour, obligations of a duty of care for which the standards should be not be diminished without careful consideration by jurists.

On the other hand, this is also a category that can more easily be misused and thus needs careful interpretation and elucidation *inter alia* to prevent it from become a 'catch-all' category used by Muslims to fight everything they subjectively may categorise as 'satanic'. The oppression of the Yazidis by ISIS in Syria and Iraqis justified on the basis that they are satanic, or, closer to home, one needs to be careful that this legal ground is not instrumentally and arbitrarily used to create problems between farmers (or others) where none now exists. It is always possible that sacred texts of faith groups are used instrumentally and Muslim jurists must pre-empt this abusive use. For example, it would appear disingenuous to use this ground to take human life, and not with standing the importance of this issue, for the protection of animal rights.

---

86. For a discussion of these issues in peace time under the *sharia*, see generally, Asmi Wood, 'Animal Welfare under the *Sharia*', *Macquarie Law Journal*, 12 (2013): 155–72.

Contemporary weapons and permitted means of fighting

While the use by Muslims fighters of relatively freely available contemporary weapons has been the practice there are some classical prohibitions that may apply to the use of these weapons, which must be considered for *sharia* legality. Necessity is a general *sharia* exception (Qur'an 2:173), and is perhaps the practical grounds on which contemporary Muslims ignore classical prohibitions. It is not evident, however, that a legal analytical process has systematically been applied to the permissibility of use of each of these contemporary weapons by Muslims. *Sharia* application of necessity requires that the objective component that circumscribes 'necessary' actions must be reasonable, just (Qur'an 16:90; Qur'an 38:26; Qur'an 55:9) and equitable (Qur'an 5:42) and will be considered using the following classical prohibition as an example.

The use of fire as a weapon

The use of fire in warfare was prohibited by the Prophet under the classical *sharia*,[87] a prohibition not known to international law. The Prophet said, that burning, described by him as 'a punishment', was reserved for God alone.[88] In 'developing' a practical position from this absolute rule, the Muslim jurists of the past turned their minds to the pressing issue of being confronted by an enemy that was not bound by this *sharia* restriction. To this end, Shafi'i, an eponym considered the head of the Shafi'i *sharia* school, states that fire may not be used *first*, but Muslims may resort to its use in case of *dire* necessity.[89] Shafi'i defined dire necessity as arising if the enemy used such weapons first or using the Prophet's precedent at Ta'if, for cutting off

---

87. al-Bukhari, *The Translations of the Meaning of Sahih al-Bukhari*, vol. 4, 161; Peters, *Jihad in Classical and Modern Islam*, 35; Khaled Abou El-Fadl, *The Great Theft: Wrestling Islam from the Extremists* (New York: Harper SanFrancisco, 2005), 55.; Hashmi, 'Islamic Ethics and Weapons of Mass Destruction', 321, 328.

88. 'Then God said to the Fire, "You are my (means of) punishment by which I punish whoever I wish of my slaves"': Muhammad Al-Mughirah al-Bukhari, *The Translations of the Meaning of Sahih al-Bukhari*, vol. 6 (Chicago: Kazi Publications, 1976), 354.

89. Abou El-Fadl, *Rebellion and Violence in Islamic Law*, 152.

all supplies, if the enemy was occupying a fortress,[90] and as a result were targeting and 'picking off' the Muslims with ease.

On the other hand, today's wars use such in discriminately destructive weapons as 5,000 or 10,000 pound, phosphorous or cluster bombs, which burn people alive, including non-combatants, and cause a relatively slow and painful death by fire over large geographical areas. However, the total prohibition on the use of fire, if promulgated, would in practice effectively outlaw the use under the *sharia* of most contemporary weapons. As the use of 'fire' in the form of gun powder, bombs and other explosive devices has become so commonplace, the *sharia* prohibition against the use of fire has been abandonedin practice by Muslims.

On the other hand, in order to avoid the unexamined abandonment of *sharia* norms Muslim jurists should examine these contemporary legal questions in detail. Developing new *sharia* norms by extending its limits to accommodate 'potent' contemporary weapons should carefully be supervised by Muslim jurists who must set clear limits on the lawful use of each 'new' permitted weapon, even if these conditions disadvantage Muslims in a military 'first strike' sense.[91] These limits could be based on an objective form of *sharia* necessity. On a related issue, jurists progressively should also identify the conditions under which Muslims may develop, test, stockpile and/or use contemporary weapons and weapons systems, including chemical and nuclear devices and other weapons which 'burn', but which are not totally prohibited under international law. (For example States, including Australia, ban the use of cluster bombs, albeit based on reasons other than solely on the basis that they 'burn' like fire).[92] Muslims should take the opportunity to use *sharia* norms to join in and

---

90. Abou El-Fadl, *Rebellion and Violence in Islamic Law*, 152.

91. Recall that the Qur'anic notion is that for Muslims, 'victory' is in God's hand alone. Another authority for this proposition is that a Muslim army is allowed to fight when it is half as numerous as that of the enemy, a clear numerical disadvantage.

92. The aim here is to have an authoritative and regularly updated text for Muslim lawyers and dealing with weapons, means, etc., in the meaning of Article 36 of AP I and without being prescriptive, something not dissimilar to the UK Ministry of Defence, *The Manual of the Law of Armed Conflict* (Oxford: Oxford University Press, 2004). The authority for the proposition that ('organic' matter or) 'chemicals' and 'nuclear' weapons can 'burn' like fire and hence included in the discussion at this point are from Qur'an 44:43 and Qur'an 24:35 respectively.

promote weapons ban treaties, particularly weapons that cause slow painful deaths to animals and humans. Bans on such weapons will hasten the crystallisation of international law. Islamic law is a juristic tradition;[93] ideally, it could also be left to the judges to draw the 'law' from the uncodified common law of Islam, as did the ICJ judges in the *Nicaragua Case*.[94] This will help in the process of developing the positive law under both systems.

The resulting legal guidance will assist Muslims to judge the legality of the means used, not only in Islamist military action, but also those of Muslim States engaged in war with each other.[95] Until new legal tests are developed, and are accepted by consensus, the long standing Shafi'i test of 'dire necessity'[96] must arguably stand as the sole legal exception to the total prohibition on the use of fire as an offensive weapon.

Further, there is no legal basis, even in the face of a huge disparity in military power, which could automatically equate with dire necessity. Clearly, as mentioned above, an exception to retaliate using fire exists if Muslims are attacked (with fire). However, if Muslims attack first, either for strategic or pre-emptive purposes the prohibition on 'first use' remains.[97] The prohibition on shedding blood must mean that Muslims should first be required to exhaust all reasonable non-coercive means of dispute resolution before resorting to the use of force and helps give meaning to the term '*fitna*' discussed above.

Until these tests are developed and articulated in positive law, Muslims must be judged under international humanitarian law as the default position, unless Islamists, as a matter of faith, are allowed to nominate the application of higher *sharia* standards. While not generalising the brutality of groups such as ISIS and Boko Haram, it is arguable that they are unlikely to accept *sharia* limits; rejection of the

---

93. Khaled Abou El-Fadl, *Speaking in God's Name: Islamic Law, Authority and Women* (Oxford: One world, 2001), 64.

94. *Case concerning the Military and Paramilitary Activities in and against Nicaragua.*

95. Some recent armed conflicts between Muslim States include the Iraq-Iran war, the Iraq-Kuwait war and the Malaysia-Indonesia conflict.

96. See above text at n. 89.

97. Please note the distinction between 'first use' even with respect to defensive war as opposed to the notion of an aggressive war. The question of over whelming military difference does not come into this calculus as Muslims are asked not to fight if the enemy is twice, or more, as strong (Qur'an 8:65).

sharia can be used to highlight their hypocrisy and the lip-service they pay to Islamic norms.

However, even when the use of force becomes lawful, the lawful use of fire should not automatically vest but the principle of only retaliating (i.e. a no first use policy) with fire should become the aspirational Muslim norm in practice, as it is in the law books. While a war that does not comply with these *sharia* requirements may nonetheless still be permissible under international law, such armed action should not be allowed to be characterised as an armed *djihad by Muslims*. This will help to divert Muslim support away from Islamists who appear to be electing IHL standards over the *sharia*, (purely) because IHL is more permissive.

Groups such as ISIS, Boko Haram and others unilaterally have carved out unprincipled and arbitrary, but legally unsubstantiated, 'legal exceptions'. These exceptions include the 'first use' of fire and other weapons which kill indiscriminately. Further, they also kill women, children and other protected persons, actions which are clearly *ultra vires* the *sharia*.[98] These crimes should not be allowed to 'hide' under the untested banner of *djihad*.

The accidental killing of innocents is not unknown with a range of military technologies from primate to 'precision'. Further, the pervasive and permissive IHL concept of intended 'collateral' deaths is not known to the *sharia*. The accidental unintended death of a person caused by a Muslim draws compensation (*diya*) under the *sharia*, but this is not a concept that has been fully abstracted to include intended the sort of collateral deaths covered by IHL, and needs to be examined in detail. On the other hand, contemporary Muslim fighters have subscribed to this non-Islamic law concept and have done so without justification under the *sharia*. Further, they have interpreted

---

98. It is not suggested that Muslims cannot make decisions out 'dire necessity' for the first use of fire against combatants. The case of use of fire in the form of weapons using gunpowder and other 'fire'-like means against combatants, while highly likely to be made out for necessity for example, is nonetheless a case that Islamists must make. Decisions, however, must be of narrow scope, and not in the broad blanket manner that 'permits' the random killing of protected classes in areas that have little or no military significance or connection. The use of fire against non-combatants, particularly against Muslims, however, is more difficult to make although this is a further issue for the Islamists. The purpose of this discussion is not to pre-empt the 'military' or practical arguments that Islamists may make.

the scope of this exception very widely in favour of causing a greater number of deaths, now extended to include causing non-combatant deaths to gain a military advantage. 'Terrorists' know that that this is clearly contrary to the *sharia* but have colluded with Islamophobes to gain mutual advantage. In Indonesia, Bali bomber Imam Samudra, who was convicted for terrorism, admitted that killing civilians was wrong and yet in his heyday with JI appeared to do so with impunity.[99] Indonesian authorities have used the confessions and remorse of contrite convicted terrorists, who had been involved in the use of force, to help change the culture among Muslim Indonesians through education and by distinguishing mayhem, carnage and cruelty caused by terrorism from that of lawful *djihad*. This educative practice should be used widely among Muslims to help reduce the present carnage and scourge that is caused by terrorism, and just as significantly the asymmetric and cruel responses to terrorism.

Harm to other (i.e. non-human) sentient beings

As indicated above, the spiritual values promoted by Islam and supported by the primary sources do not exclude kindness and care for sentient animals.[100] The authority for this proposition of kindness to animals comes from a *hadith* (paraphrased below):

> It was narrated from the Prophet that a prostitute [in one version, a man] came upon a well in the desert [on the edge of an oasis] to have a drink. She saw a dog licking the mud to quench its excessive thirst. After she had her drink, she thought, 'this dog is suffering as much as I did', so she filled her shoe with water, and gave the dog a drink. God Most Merciful thanked the prostitute and forgave her all her previous sins. So the people asked the Prophet: 'O God's Apostle, is there a reward for us for serving the animals? The Prophet replied, '(Yes.) There is a reward [from God] for serving any animate being [living thing].'[101]

---

99.   Michael Sheridan, 'We Didn't Mean to Kill So Many: Bomber', *The Australian* (Melbourne) (3 March 2008).

100.   Asad, *The Message of the Qur'an*, 190.

101.   Muhammad Al-Mughirah al-Bukhari, *The Translations of the Meaning of Sahih al-Bukhari*, vol. 8 (Chicago: Kazi Publications, 1976), 25.

The prohibition on animal cruelty was also shown above with respect to the treatment of the pet cat, the slitting of ears and the cutting of limbs. These prohibitions apply generally and so in principle should apply to combat situations for example in times when animals were used in combat. These rules and laws should also be appropriately adapted to consider prohibitions against the reckless collateral killing and maiming of people, animals and damage to the environment.

Conclusion

This is a very brief examination of the *sharia* laws related to the use of force touching on environmental and animal welfare. Much of the law in the area remains undeveloped in the *sharia* jurisprudence and there is an urgent need for this law to be examined and made contemporary, ready for application. Until this happens many contemporary Muslim fighters are likely to continue to claim that they are engaged in a 'holy' war (*djihad*) while in practice ignoring the tenets of their faith's basic laws of conducting lawful warfare. Some Muslims have unjustifiably ignored or abandoned their own laws mostly for instrumental reasons. It is concluded that the urgent, principled development of *sharia* laws on the use of force would be beneficial to humankind and the others who share this planet with us.

'Oil and Blood on the Bayonet': Empire, Oil, War and Ecology

Mick Pope

The title of this essay comes from the song 'What are we Fighting for?'[1] This final song on Live's 2003 album *Birds of Pray* explains the perceived connection between oil and geopolitics, particularly U.S. foreign policy. This essay examines the connection between oil, empire and war in pursuit of oil. The continued use of oil as an energy source is not an ecological good, and therefore the building of empire based on the aggressive acquisition of this resource is morally wrong. By examining oil driven conflicts, this essay describes a positive feedback loop in the climate system. After examining the basics of oil, I will look at oil history and why in particular the U.S. has become so dependent upon oil, and how this dependence has influenced their foreign policy, particularly in the Middle East. I focus on the U.S. primarily because it was the first nation to centre its economy on oil and because it dominates current global consumption. I then consider two conflicts involving oil: Iraq and East Timor. Oil imperialism will then be examined by considering Paul's critique of empire in Romans.

Oil basics

Conventional crude oil is a complex set of hydrocarbons that can be pumped out of the ground and refined into more useful forms. Oil was formed between 200 and 2.5 million years ago via the breakdown of organic (carbon-based) marine matter. Combustion releases this fossil carbon back into the atmosphere, contributing to the accumu-

---

1. Patrick Dahlheimer, Chad Alan Gracey, Edward Joel Kowalczyk, Chad David Taylor, 'What Are We Fighting For?' (Mucho Loco Music, 2003).

lation of CO_2 and resulting climate change.[2] Oil is the second largest contributor to global green house gas emissions.[3] It is estimated that to have a 50% chance of keeping the global average temperature below 2°C above the pre-industrial average by the end of the century, approximately a third of known oil reserves will need to be left unused.[4]

Petroleum accounts for 97% of all transport fuel used in the U.S., and is 'the most versatile fuel source ever discovered, situated at the core of the modern industrial economy'.[5] Apart from transport, oil is used in plastics, synthetic fibres and a variety of chemicals. The U.S. was the first country in the world to develop a large scale petroleum industry in 1859 and relies on oil more than any other nation for its military.[6] Oil is important because of its high energy density and its transportability. It is therefore difficult and costly to substitute, given existing economic needs and infrastructure.[7] In particular, oil is not easily substituted in transportation without the right policies or price incentives. There is resistance to tax increases that will change consumption and the sense of entitlement to cheap oil. The U.S. economy is critically dependent upon cheap oil because oil in security, as Gavin Bridge and Phillipe Le Billon comment 'derives historically from wastage and shortsightedness of an "Age of Plenty" that considered oil the lubricant of infinite growth'.[8]

Oil reserves are unevenly distributed across the planet, with 54% of proven reserves being found in the Middle East.[9] This means that 'the Persian Gulf remains the epicentre of energy geopolitics'.[10] Peak oil is the phenomenon that conventional oil reserves reach a peak

---

2. Gavin Bridge and Philippe Le Billon, *Oil* (Cambridge: Polity Press, 2013), 6.

3. James Hansen *et al*, 'Assessing "Dangerous Climate Change": Required Reduction of Carbon Emissions to Protect Young People, Future Generations and Nature', *PLOS One* (3 December 2013), <http://journals.plos.org/plosone/article?id=10.1371/journal.pone.0081648>. Accessed 23 August 2015.

4. Christophe McGlade and Paul Ekins, 'The Geographical Distribution of Fossil Fuels Unused when Limiting Global Warming to 2 C', *Nature* 517 (2015): 187–90.

5. Edward L Morse, 'A New Political Economy of Oil?', *Journal of International Affairs* 53/1 (Fall 1999): 2.

6. Michael Klare, *Blood and Oil* (London: Penguin Books, 2005), 8.

7. Bridge and Le Billon, *Oil*, 101.

8. Bridge and Le Billon, *Oil*, 101.

9. Bridge and Le Billon, *Oil*, 11.

10. Bridge and Le Billon, *Oil*, 93.

in extraction rate, before declining to terminal levels of production. In 1956, Shell geologist M King Hubbert correctly predicted that American oil output (excluding Alaska) would peak in the 1970s, based on the production trends of oil reservoirs. Oil output can be described using a bell curve, where output rises until the reservoir is half empty and then drops just as quickly. This is due to the reservoir losing its 'geological vigor'.[11] The pressure that initially forces oil up to the surface declines over time, and hence the oil can become more difficult to extract. Secondary efforts like pumping water or gas are then required. It is also possible to damage a reservoir by pumping oil out too quickly, and the output might collapse before the reserve is exhausted.[12] This risk is very real, because demand for oil rises every year, and fields like those in Saudi Arabia are under pressure to increase output.[13]

Oil history

British interest in Middle Eastern oil goes back at least to its involvement in Anglo-Persian Oil in 1914.[14] During the Great War, oil changed the nature of warfare with the introduction of tanks by Winston Churchill, the use of aeroplanes and the shift from coal to oil in the British Naval fleet.[15] Baghdad was 'liberated' by Britain from the Ottoman Empire in 1917. The League of Nations recognised the new country of Iraq and placed it under British rule. Iraq achieved quasi-independence in 1932 but British troops remained because of oil.[16] Before 1951, Iranian oil was extracted by the Anglo-Iranian Oil Company, with most of the taxes paid to London while most Iranians lived in poverty. In 1951, Iran's parliament nationalised the company and British boycotts soon followed. Once Eisenhower became U.S. president, the British were able to get the U.S. to instigate a coup under

11. Peter Maass, *Crude World: The Violent Twilight of Oil* (London: Allen Lane, 2009), 13.
12. Maass, *Crude World*, 16–17.
13. Maass, *Crude World*, 23.
14. Daniel Yergin, *The Prize: The Epic Quest for Oil, Money and Power* (New York: Touchstone, 1992), 173.
15. Yergin, *The Prize*, 168–72.
16. Maass, *Crude World*, 149.

the threat that Iran would support the Soviets. In 1953, the Shah was installed as leader with the help of the CIA.[17]

The U.S. was the world's leading oil producer from 1860 until it entered WWII in 1942. The U.S. fuelled its huge military effort and that of its allies to such an extent that projections suggested that reserves would be depleted in 13 years. This led to a 'more aggressive foreign oil policy aimed at assuring access to petroleum overseas.'[18] Oil was struck in Saudi Arabia in 1938 by the Standard Oil Company of California and production began the following year. In 1943, Roosevelt declared Saudi oil to be vital to the defence of the USA and hence the country a worthy recipient of U.S. aid. By 1945, Saudi Arabia's oil reserves were recognised as 'a stupendous source of strategic power, and one of the greatest material prizes in human history.'[19]

Today, petroleum dependency has created the situation whereby the U.S. economy and military has dominated the world, but to grow further requires imported oil. At 5% of the global population, the U.S. consumes about 25% of the global oil supply.[20] Policies under Truman, Eisenhower and Nixon saw increasing military aid to Saudi Arabia.[21] With threats in the region of Soviets in Afghanistan and the fall of the Shah in Iran, the Carter Doctrine (1980) promised that

> an attempt by any outside force to gain control of the Persian
> Gulf region will be regarded as an assault on the vital interests
> of the United States of America, and such an assault with be
> repelled by any means necessary, including military force.[22]

Reagan extended this doctrine to support rebels in the overthrow of the Soviets in Afghanistan. Pledging ongoing support to keep the oil coming out of Saudi Arabia, the U.S. also provided support to Iraq in

---

17. Maass, *Crude World*, 143–4.
18. Andrew F Carter to Max Thornberg, 'Project for a Study of U.S. Foreign Oil Policy' (24 November 1941), cited in Klare, *Blood and Oil*, 29–30.
19. Dean Acheson, 'Draft Memorandum to President Truman' (undated), cited in 'Foreign Relations of the United States: Diplomatic Papers, 1945, The Near East and Africa', Volume VIII (Washington: Office of the Historian, 1945), <https:// history.state.gov/historicaldocuments/frus1945v08/d20>. Accessed 14 October, 2016.
20. Klare, *Blood and Oil*, 11.
21. Klare, *Blood and Oil*, 43.
22. Jimmy Carter, cited in Maass, *Crude World*, 142.

its war against Iran. The Iranian Islamic revolution could not afford to be repeated in Saudi Arabia. This policy changed when Iraq attacked Kuwait, signalling a threat to Saudi oil supplies and hence U.S. interests.[23] The U.S. thought ground troops in Saudi Arabia were the best way of protecting the country and royal family, but this was a reversal of a long standing policy of not allowing 'infidels' near some of the holiest sites in Islam. This offending of Islamic sensibilities resulted in Bin Laden's campaign against the royal family and the U.S.[24]

Recent oil imperialism

The U.S. invasion of Iraq

Although George W Bush recognised in 1998 that there was a U.S. energy crisis, his placing Dick Cheney, a former CEO of the oil field service company Halliburton, in charge did not bode well. Cheney stated that 'Conservation may be a sign or personal virtue, but it is not a sufficient basis for sound, comprehensive energy policy.'[25] While Bush made pledges to stop reliance on foreign oil, the U.S. military continued to play a key role as part of his energy policy.[26] His policy on energy dated back to the early 90s and the Defensive Planning Guidance which aimed at blocking 'European-only security arrangements' that marginalised the U.S. The U.S. should 'remain the dominant outside power in the region and preserve U.S. and Western access to the region's oil'.[27] This policy was denounced both in congress and around with the world, with Democrat Joe Biden declaring it 'nothing but a Pax Americana'.[28] Indeed, the outcome of this policy was a melding

---

23. Klare, *Blood and Oil*, 48–9.
24. Klare, *Blood and Oil*, 52.
25. Cited in Joseph Kahn, 'Cheney Promotes Increasing Supply as Energy Policy', *New York Times* (1 May 2001), <http://www.nytimes.com/2001/05/01/us/cheney-promotes-increasing-supply-as-energy-policy.html>. Accessed 23 November 2016.
26. Klare, *Blood and Oil*, 15.
27. From a leaked section of a document printed in the *New York Times*, cited in Klare, *Blood and Oil*, 68.
28. Cited in Melissa Healy, 'Global Role: Planning Document Outlines Strategy for Facing Challenges to American Influence', *Los Angeles Times* (9 March 1992), <http://articles.latimes.com/1992-03-09/news/mn-2561_1_united-states>. Accessed 23 November 2016.

of two White House priorities: reigning in rogue states and capturing oil and gas fields.[29] The second Gulf war should be understood in this context.

The U.S. government denied that the invasion of Iraq was tied to oil.[30] However, the Ministry of Oil was protected while everything else—including the priceless treasures of the National Museum—was looted.[31] The message to Iraq is was clear; as one Iraqi ministry official observed: 'The Americans will not steal the oil but they will control it; they will pull the strings.'[32] Saddam Hussein's actions in Kuwait were perceived as a threat to American oil hegemony. Invading Kuwait—a usally—would give him control of one quarter of oil reserves in the world, and threaten Saudi Arabia. Dick Cheney echoed this concern, commenting that:

> [Saddam] has clearly done what he has to do to dominate OPEC, the Gulf and the Arab world. He is forty kilometres from Saudi Arabia and its oil production is only a couple of hundred kilometres away. If he doesn't take it physically, with his new wealth he will still have an impact and will be able to acquire new weapons.[33]

The now clearly false accusations of weapons of mass destruction was also linked with oil:

> Armed with an arsenal of these weapons of terror, and seated atop ten percent of the world's oil reserves, Saddam Hussein could then be expected to seek domination of the world's energy supplies.[34]

The official U.S. justification for invasion was concern about, as George HW Bush claimed, 'a world where the rule of law supplants the rule of the jungle'.[35] Yet this principle was applied selectively; in many places where the 'rule of the jungle' was allowed to continue,

---

29. Klare, *Blood and Oil*, 70.
30. Maass, *Crude World*, 5.
31. Maass, *Crude World*, 8.
32. Cited in Maass, *Crude World*, 137.
33. Cited in Maass, *Crude World*, 140.
34. Cited in Maass, *Crude World*, 160.
35. Cited in Maass, *Crude World*, 146.

but where there was no oil.[36] Indeed, the U.S. had long supported Hussein and his tyrannical rule. Likewise, Noam Chomsky claims that the U.S. attitude toward the U.N. and formation of the 'coalition of the willing', together with their disdain of 'Old Europe', highlight that this invasion was not about the upholding of democratic principles.[37] Instead, the invasion was the rolling out of a prepared strategy. One month before the liberation of Kuwait, National Security Directive 54 was issued by George Bush:

> Access to Persian Gulf oil and the security of key friendly states in the area are vital to U.S. national security. The United States remains committed to defending its vital interests in the region, if necessary through the use of military force, against any power with interests inimical to our own.[38]

The U.S. has preferred to deal with dictators. In 2004, prominent oilmen warned that war in Iraq would destabilise supplies. However, Ryszard Kapuściński observed that oil tends to induce a form of madness that 'anesthetizes thought, blurs vision, corrupts'.[39] Hence, while invading Iraq was not logical from the point of view of a steady supply of oil, the invasion displays the spell oil casts on empire in its desire to gain control over resources.

Australia and East Timor

Australia has not engaged in warfare directly to acquire oil, but it has benefitted from violence, has been a 'liberator' with mixed motives and has engaged in espionage in its dealings with East Timor. In doing so, as Kim McGrath observes, 'for more than 40 years, Australia has played hardball with some of the poorest people on earth'.[40] Onshore

---

36. E.g. in Liberia; Maass, *Crude World*, 146.
37. Noam Chomsky, *Hegemony or Survival: America's Quest for Global Dominance* (Crow's Nest, NSW: Allen and Unwin, 2003), ch 5.
38. Cited in Maass, *Crude World*, 147.
39. Ryszard Kapuściński, *Shah of Shahs* (New York: Vintage International, 1992), cited in Maass, *Crude World*, 159.
40. Kim McGrath, 'Oil, Gas, and Spy Games in the Timor Sea: Australian Scheming for the Greater Sunrise Oil field has a Long History', *The Monthly* (April 2014), <https://www.themonthly.com.au/issue/2014/april/1396270800/kim-mcgrath/oil-gas-and-spy-games-timor-sea>. Accessed 24 February 2015.

drilling in East Timor by Australian companies began with Timor Oil in 1956, and continued with BHP until 1975, when the political situation deteriorated.[41] Timor Oil sold their concession to Wood side who began exploration offshore between Timor and Australia. At the time, the *Northern Territory News* noted that: 'Nobody would worry about the actual granting of the permit to prospect but the situation might be radically different if the company struck oil.' During 1974, Wood side found oil and named the field 'Greater Sunrise'.[42]

Timor was split between the western half under Indonesian control, and the east which was a Portuguese colony. The Australian Government maintained that its maritime sovereignty extended to the edge of the continental shelf, which they claimed was more than two thirds of the way to Timor.[43] This was due to a supposed plate boundary referred to as the Timor Trough. In reality, the trough is more of a wrinkle and Timor is part of the same tectonic plate.[44] According to international maritime law, the proper boundary lies halfway between Timor and Australia. Portugal disputed Australia's claim at the time, but Indonesian president Suharto was more amenable to agreement, and granted Australia a large area above the median line. The dispute with Portugal left a gap in the boundary line between Portuguese Timor and Australia, the so-called Timor Gap.[45] Australian sovereignty over Greater Sunrise could not be guaranteed until this gap was closed.

A revolution in Portugal provided an opportunity for this gap to be closed, as all of its former colonies were granted independence. In December 1975 Indonesia invaded East Timor, and Australia did not voice its opposition. The primary reason for Australian acceptance of the invasion appears to be a concern for regional stability. Gough Whitlam noted Indonesian concern that the East Timorese revolu-

---

41. James Dunn, *Timor: A People Betrayed* (Sydney: ABC Books, 1996), 42.

42. Cited in Gordon Peake, *Beloved Land: Stories, Struggles, and Secrets from Timor-Leste* (Melbourne: Scribe, 2013), 181.

43. McGrath, *Oil, Gas and Spy Games in the Timor Sea.*

44. Paul Cleary, *Shakedown: Australia's Grab for Timor Oil* (Crow's Nest: Allen and Unwin, 2007), 7–9.

45. McGrath, *Oil, Gas and Spy Games in the Timor Sea.*

tionary party Fretilin were communist.[46] Whitlam himself believed that stability in the region would be best served by Timor being incorporated into Indonesia, but with the approval of the people.[47] This approval apparently did not extend to the Fretilin Government established after internal conflict, with Richard Woolcott, Australian Ambassador to Indonesia stating in September 1975 that Australia's interests would be best served by Timor's association with Indonesia rather than independence.[48] This Australian interest was expressed by Woolcott in a communication to Canberra in August 1975:

> The present gap in the agreed seabed border ... could be much more readily negotiated with Indonesia ... than with Portugal or an independent Portuguese Timor. I know I am recommending a pragmatic rather than a principled stand but that is what the national interest and foreign policy is all about.[49]

Hence, while the Australian Government at the time did not support the invasion for the purposes of obtaining Timorese oil, nor did they condone Indonesian violence, they did seek to gain from the situation.

International pressure further weakened any concern Australia could have had for the situation. While in opposition, Malcolm Fraser seems to have believed in the risk of a communist Fretilin.[50] He later appears to have opposed the violence, with foreign Minister Alexander Peacock developing a policy that called for the withdrawals of troops and a genuine act of self-determination.[51] The U.S. State Department in 1976 called on Australian Prime Minister Malcolm Fraser to weaken his negative stance toward Indonesia, as both countries were seen as having political and strategic value. Good relationships with Indonesia soon became apparently more important than human rights and autonomy in East Timor. This included seizing a radio transmitter in Darwin which had been receiving signals from

---

46. Commonwealth of Australia, *East Timor: Final Report of the Senate Foreign Affairs, Defence and Trade References Committee* (Canberra: Senate Printing Unit, Parliament House, Canberra, 2000), 130.
47. Commonwealth of Australia, *East Timor*, 123.
48. Commonwealth of Australia, *East Timor*, 129.
49. Woolcott, cited in Peake, *Beloved Land*, 183.
50. Commonwealth of Australia, *East Timor*, 132.
51. Commonwealth of Australia, *East Timor*, 152.

Fretilin about conditions in Timor, and later making apology for the invasion as necessary.[52] By 1978, considerations of the situation in Timor appeared focussed on the need, as James Dunn notes, to 'negotiate the demarcation of the seabed boundary between Indonesia's latest acquisition and Australia'. Dunn also criticises the hypocrisy of the Australia Government calling for an end to foreign aggression in Poland, Afghanistan and South Africa, while describing the 1991 Santa Cruz massacre of 250 demonstrators in East Timor as an aberration.[53] Such a stance does not suggest Australia approved of the violence, but viewed it less negatively than other foreign situations.

Negotiations with Indonesia and Australia dragged on until 1989, when the Timor Gap Treaty was signed, granting Australia more than 80% of Greater Sunrise. While Australia played a key role in restoring order after the Indonesian withdrawal from East Timor, it has continued to lay claim to its oil. Upon independence, the U.N. locked Timor into the same boundary. When Australia withdrew from the maritime boundary jurisdiction of the International Court of Justice, East Timor was forced into further negotiations, led by foreign affairs minister Alexander Downer. He would later go on to be a lobbyist for Wood side. The 2006 treaty increased Timor's share of revenue to 50% of the whole field but the boundaries remained unchanged and not open to negotiation for 50 years, by which times reserves would be depleted. Australia walked away with the rights to billions of dollars that belonged rightfully to East Timor.[54]

On top of these heavy handed negotiations, Australia engaged in espionage during the 2004 negotiations. A former Australian Secret Intelligence Service agent had reportedly provided an affidavit alleging that bugging had occurred in order to secure commercial advantage for Australia during the treaty negotiations. This agent had his passport confiscated, preventing him from travelling to The Hague, where the Permanent Court of Arbitration was hearing Timor's application to have the 2004 treaty overturned. Meanwhile, Australian Security Intelligence Organisation and the Australian Federal Police confiscated files belonging to a lawyer representing Timor in the dispute. Prime Minister Tony Abbott meanwhile claims that Australia

---

52. Dunn, *Timor*, 343–4.
53. Dunn, *Timor*, 346–8.
54. McGrath, *Oil, Gas and Spy Games in the Timor Sea*.

uses surveillance 'to protect our citizens and the citizens of other countries, and we certainly don't use it for commercial purposes'.[55] More recently, the Permanent Court of Arbitration in the Hague has agreed to adjudicate in the dispute, a decision the Australian Government had argued against.[56]

Empire

In the previous section, I examined the history of oil geopolitics in the Middle East, and traced modern activity by the U.S. in Iraq and Australian involvement in East Timor. In what follows, I will offer a critique of such oil imperialism based on a theology of empire.

Defining empire

G John Ikenberry defines empire as 'the political control by a dominant country of the domestic and foreign policies of weaker countries', and hence claims the USA has never acted in an imperial fashion.[57] Martin Walker disagrees, suggesting that empire is 'a metaphor rather than a precise definition'.[58] Walker defines empire 'by the challenges they choose to confront', in particular by the dictum 'Trade without rule where possible; trade with rule where necessary' and identifies past British and present U.S. activities in this light. Brian Walsh and Sylvia Keesmaat define empire as the

> systematic centralizations of power and secured by structures of socio-economic and military control. They are religiously legitimated by powerful myths that are rooted in foundational assumptions, and they are sustained by a proliferation

55. Quoted in an ABC radio interview, cited in McGrath, *Oil, Gas and Spy Games in the Timor Sea*.

56. Australian Broadcasting Corporation, 'Global Court Agrees to Take Up Timor, Australia Sea Border Row', *ABC News* (27 September 2016), <http://www.abc. net.au/news/2016-09-27/court-of-arbitration-takes-up-australia-timor-sea-border-row/7879286>. Accessed 12 October 2016.

57. Cited in Arthur Schlessinger Jr, 'The American Empire? Not so Fast', *World Policy Journal* (Spring 2005): 43–6.

58. Martin Walker, 'America's Virtual Empire', *World Policy Journal* (Winter, 2002): 13–20.

of imperial symbols that capture the imagination of the populace.[59]

This last definition recognises the complex socio-economic and religious mythology underpinning empire. Key is the centralisation of power but absent is the need for an accompanying colonialism. Finally, Richard Horsley lists military power, colonisation, indirect rule through client states or alliances with aristocracies or oligarchies, and cultural imperialism as key factors.[60]

Some biblical scholars seek to down play the significance of the rhetoric of empire, suggesting that certain biblical texts are ambivalent in their treatment.[61] It may be true that we will always have empires, but this does not obviate our need to live out the gospel and do justice in such contexts. Indeed, the context of empire gives shape to our doing justice. As Lillian Daniel observes, both Testaments 'were forged under the white-hot pressures of real-world empires'.[62] Horsley adds that much of Scripture 'is closely connected with imperial power relations'.[63] I now turn to the text of Rom 1, in particular to studying the language of empire, its symbols and structures, in the 1st century world, before applying this to 21st century oil geopolitics.

Rome as empire

JS Richardson notes that 'The secular activity of the Roman state … in the period of the republic may be summarized in two words: war and law, and that war 'was the context not only of the acquisition but also of the establishment of what became the Roman territorial

---

59. Brian J Walsh and Sylvia C Keesmaat, *Colossians Remixed: Subverting the Empire* (Downers Grove, IL: Inter-Varsity Press, 2004).

60. Richard A. Horsley, *Religion and Empire: People, Power and the Life of the Spirit* (Minneapolis: Fortress, 2003), 6.

61. See for example, Andy Crouch, 'Foreword', in *Jesus is Lord Caesar is Not: Evaluating Empire in New Testament Studies*, edited by Scott McKnight and Joseph B Modica (Downers Grove, IL: IVP Academic, 2013), 161

62. Lillian Daniel, 'Empire's Sleepy Embrace', in *Anxious about Empire: Theological Essays on the New Global Realities*, edited by Wes Avram (Grand Rapids: Brazos Press, 2004), 174.

63. Horsley, *Religion and Empire*, 4.

empire'.[64] The maintenance of the so-called Pax Romana was achieved through violence, where dissent and resistance were crushed with ruthless efficiency.[65] This was the main focus of the foreign policy of the Roman senate.[66] Furthermore, as JA North notes, many Romans, including all those who had a major influence on policy decisions, knew they made large profits out of warfare and the expansion of the Empire.[67]

The link with profit is interesting. Keith Hopkins suggests tentatively that the Empire was split into a threefold military/taxation structure.[68] First was the outer ring of frontier provinces in which defensive armies were stationed. Second was the inner ring of relatively rich tax-exporting provinces, such as Spain, southern Gaul, and so on. Third, Rome was the seat of the central government, which, together with the armies, consumed a large volume of taxes. This meant that Rome lived in luxury while the rest of the empire lived in relative or actual poverty.[69] Many farmers were dispossessed of their land to become peasant tenants.[70] At the same time, Hopkins suggests that the heavy taxation of Rome increased trade. In order to pay taxes, goods were exported, largely to Rome and the frontier armies.[71] Hopkins concludes that this

> implies an increased monetization of the Roman economy, the commercialization of exchange, an elongation of the links between producers and consumers, the growth of specialist intermediaries (traders, shippers, bankers), and an unprecedented level of urbanization.[72]

---

64. JS Richardson, 'Imperium Romanum: Empire and the Language of Power', *The Journal of Roman Studies*, 81 (1991): 1–9.

65. NT Wright, *The New Testament and the People of God* (London: SPCK, 1992), 154.

66. Richardson, 'Imperium Romanum', 2.

67. JA North, 'Development of Roman Imperialism', *The Journal of Roman Studies*, 71 (1981): 1–9.

68. Keith Hopkins, 'Taxes and Trade in the Roman Empire (200 B.C.-A.D. 400)', *The Journal of Roman Studies*, 70 (1980): 101–25.

69. Wright, *The New Testament and the People of God*, 154.

70. Walsh and Keesmaat, *Colossians Remixed*, 52.

71. Hopkins, 'Taxes and Trade', 101.

72. Hopkins, 'Taxes and Trade', 102.

The link between imperial might and monetary influence is even greater when the Roman coinage is considered. Roman coinage had a persuasive function. The imperial head was a source of powerful persuasion, as the discussion in the Gospels makes clear (for example, Mk 12:13–17).[73] The coinage distributed the image of the remote ruler to the far corners of the Empire. The emperor's head is a symbol of the central power of the state and the coinage points to a power beyond itself and draws its validity from that power.[74] A conventional contrast before the 50s was that the obverse is occupied by the head of a god.[75] In the time of the early church, the image was of Pax, the goddess of peace on one side, with weapons on the other.[76] The linking of religion, war and violence, peace and economics could not be clearer.

In this context, it is possible to understand Paul's declaration of the gospel in Rom 1:1–5 as anti-empire by presenting Jesus as the world's true Lord in contradistinction to Caesar. It matters little whether or not Romans is intended by Paul to be a 'political manifesto' or a 'pastoral theology', as such a distinction is less useful in a context where there are always socio-political implications of the faith of Israel.[77] What is important is that Paul is writing to house churches living in the city of Rome, the centre of empire. That, as we shall see, his language deliberately echoes that of empire, strongly suggests that his intention was to remind his readers of the superior nature of the Lordship of Christ, and their unity as both Jew and Gentile under that Lordship (see for example Rom 1:16; 2:9–10; 10:12).

The parallels in language between Paul and empire are made clear through an examination of an inscription from 9BCE regarding Augustus:

> The *providence* which has ordered the whole of our life,
> showing concern and zeal, has ordained the most perfect

---

73. Andrew Wallace-Hadrill, 'Image and Authority in the Coinage of Augustus', *The Journal of Roman Studies*, 76 (1986): 66–87, 68.

74. Wallace-Hadrill, 'Image and Authority', 69–70.

75. Wallace-Hadrill, 'Image and Authority', 74.

76. Walsh and Keesmaat, *Colossians Remixed*, 52.

77. Michael F Bird, 'One Who Will Arise to Rule Over the Nations: Paul's Letter to Romans and the Roman Empire', in *Jesus is Lord Caesar is Not: Evaluating Empire in New Testament Studies*, edited by Scott McKnight and Joseph B Modica (Downers Grove, IL: IVP Academic, 2013), 161.

> consummation for human life by giving to it Augustus, by filling him with virtue for doing the work of a benefactor among men, and by sending in him, as it were, a *savior* for us and those who come after us, to make *war to cease*, to create order everywhere …; the birthday of the *god* [Augustus] was the beginning for the world of the *glad tidings* that have come to men through him …(emphasis added).[78]

First, note the claim that the birthday of Augustus is glad tidings (*euangelion*). Isaiah 40 identifies *euangelion* with the forgiveness of Israel's sins; Israel's return from exile represents God's showing up the idols of the nations (Isa 40:19–20). Given this Old Testament association, of God's good news versus idols, it is not surprising that Paul's announcement of the gospel (Rom 1:1–3) strongly suggests an implicit critique of Rome. Secondly, Christ means Messiah or anointed king. Paul as an apostle of King Jesus is his herald, announcing his reign. In Rom 1:3, Paul describes Jesus as descended from David according to the flesh, that is, the Davidic king (2 Sam 7:12–16). Thirdly, as Son of God Jesus is both Messiah and divine man.[79] The Messiah is God's son (Ps 2), his anointed king who will rule the nations and in whom the rulers of the nations should take refuge. As Son of God, Jesus has a divine lineage to challenge the claims of the Caesars.[80]

The resurrection is central to understanding Jesus as Son of God in the messianic sense. The first century world was full of would be Messiahs, and once they had been executed by Rome their followers went looking for another Messiah. In being crucified, Jesus was merely another failed Messiah, but in being raised from the dead, he was vindicated and shown to be the true Messiah (Rom 1:4). Further more, many of Jesus' words and deeds identified him closely with Israel's God. As the unique Son of God Jesus stands in contrast to the false claims of divinity by Augustus. Peace with God comes through the Lord Jesus Christ and his death (Rom 5:1–11) whereas the Pax Romana, was kept by obeying Roman law. One is liberating, the other enslaving.

---

78. Cited in Tom Wright, *What Saint Paul Really Said* (Oxford: Lion Publishing, 1997), 43.

79. Thomas R. Schreiner, *Romans: Baker Exegetical Commentary on the New Testament* (Grand Rapids: Baker Books, 1998), 38.

80. Bird, 'One Who Will Arise to Rule over the Nations', 155.

If we accept that Paul is presenting the rule of Jesus as Lord in direct contradistinction to that of Caesar, then it is possible to understand Paul's statement about creation groaning and longing to be set free from bondage in Rom 8:19–23 as referring to human misrule.[81] Paul's claim that creation is groaning in birth pains stands in direct opposition to the poet Horace's claimed about Augustus that 'Thine age, O Caesar, has brought back fertile crops to the fields.'[82] The reality was quite different and much of it evident to first century observers.

First, Rome was responsible for significant deforestation, which in turn affected Caesar's so-called fertile crops.[83] Deforestation was the result of timber harvesting for construction and metal smelting.[84] Wood was also used for war:

> not only for ships but also for chariots, battering rams, and other huge siege engines, and stock for a host of weapons. Ramparts of fortifications often consisted of tree trunks set closely together. Armies took their toll upon the forests.[85]

Erosion was widespread in ancient Rome and Greece, as well as microclimate change, leading to a decline in agricultural production.[86]

Secondly, life in Rome was affected by environmental mismanagement. Through a complex chain of physical causation, deforestation led to an increase in malarial infections, as well as flooding, river mouth silting and soil erosion in the vicinity of Rome.[87] Air quality in Rome was poor and posed a health problem. The philosopher and senator Seneca noted that the air quality was oppressive. His health was impacted negatively; he comments that on leaving the city: 'I

---

81. See Mick Pope, 'With Heads Craning Forward: The Eschaton and the Nonhuman Creation in Romans 8', in *Ecotheology in the Humanities: An Interdisciplinary Approach to Understanding the Divine and Nature*, edited by Melissa J. Brotton (Lanham, MD: Lexington Books, 2016).

82. Walsh and Keesmaat, *Colossians Remixed*, 54.

83. Lara O'Sullivan, Andrew Jardine, Angus Cook and Philip Weinstein, 'Deforestation, Mosquitoes, and Ancient Rome: Lessons for Today', *Bioscience* 58 (2008): 756–60.

84. J Donald Hughes and JV Thirgood, 'Deforestation, Erosion, and Forest Management in Ancient Greece and Rome', *Journal of Forest History* 26 (1982): 60–75.

85. Hughes and Thirgood, 'Deforestation, Erosion, and Forest Management', 64.

86. Hughes and Thirgood, 'Deforestation, Erosion, and Forest Management', 68–9.

87. O'Sullivan *et al*, 'Deforestation, Mosquitoes, and Ancient Rome', 757.

noticed the change in my condition at once.'[88] Likewise, aqueducts brought water in from a distance, as the River Tiber was used as a sewer. The Tiber was connected to Rome's drainage system via the Cloaca Maximus. The river must have then been 'seriously polluted and frequently malodorous'.[89]

Oil geopolitics and empire

I have argued that oil has played a key role in the geopolitics of the Middle East, and Australian-Indonesian-Timorese relationships. I have shown that empire can be defined as the political control of weaker nations via socio-economics and military might. Control of trade is key, with a net inward flow of resources to the centre of empire. In contrast, the gospel offers an alternative narrative, with Paul's announcement of the gospel in Rom 1:1–5 showing Caesar to be a false god and lord. True peace comes through Jesus not the Pax Romana (Rom 5:8) or Pax Americana, and the rhetoric of empire-driven progress is empty (Rom 8:20–21). What now remains is to make the necessary links and provide a gospel-shaped alternative. Caution needs to be applied in such comparisons. Michael Bird notes that many anti-imperial readings of Romans have arisen at a time of anti-American sentiment.[90] Nonetheless, for Romans at least, there does appear to be a critique of empire given the context of Paul's readers. If, further, there are close similarities between Rome and the contemporary U.S. for example, it may be a case of 'if the shoe fits'.

Control of access to Middle Eastern oil has been Western policy for many decades, if not centuries. This has included joint control of oil companies, military occupation or support of dictatorships. It has formed part of the explicit doctrine of several U.S. presidents. One aspect of first century Roman policy in Palestine was the use of vassals. Herod the Great was Rome's ruler in Jerusalem.[91] Annas the high

---

88. Stephen Mosley, 'Environmental History of Air Pollution and Protection', in *The Basic Environmental History*, edited by Mauro Agnoletti and Simone Neri Serneri (Heidelberg: Springer, 2014), 145.

89. Brian Campbell, *Rivers and the Power of Ancient Rome* (Chapel Hill: The University of North Carolina Press, 2012), 239.

90. Bird, 'One Who Will Arise to Rule over the Nations', 148–9.

91. Wright, *The New Testament and the People of God*, 160.

priest and his successors were chosen by Rome. Likewise, as Peter Maass notes, the U.S. government does not buy or transport foreign oil but instead 'tries to ensure that oil reserves are controlled by friendly governments and friendly companies that will extract and transport steady supplies of oil,'[92] and it ensures that the infrastructure exists to get the oil to the U.S. Navy patrols in the Persian Gulf ensure the safety of supertankers, so much so that the U.S. military 'has been called an oil-protection service'.[93] In cases like Saddam Hussein (pre-Kuwait) or the Saudis, U.S. governments are willing to tolerate dictatorial rule so long as its vassals maintain the supply of oil. However, just as Rome had eventually to remove Archelaus for his extreme violence and ineptness, the U.S. was willing to over throw Hussein when he became uncontrollable, not as regards his treatment of his own people but in relation to what America considered rightfully theirs, oil.[94]

While oil companies can act as the vassals of the U.S. government, in Nigeria the state acts as a vassal to the demands of big oil. As an example of the so-called resource curse, the Niger Delta in Nigeria contains a large oil reserve but its benefits are poorly distributed. In 2009, Nigeria was the eighth largest exporter of oil in the world and yet 90% of its citizens were living on less than $US2 per day, with people in the Niger Delta not properly recompensed for loss of land, poisoning of water supplies, and so on.[95] Predictably this has led to armed rebellion, which first began in 1966. While this was put down quickly by government forces, they were understood to have acted on behalf of Shell, that is, as Shell's vassal. Government forces were provided with boats by Shell. Ken Saro-Wiwa, a leader of a non-violent protest movement who was killed in 1994 believed: 'This is it, they are going to arrest us all and execute us. All for Shell.'[96] While it is unlikely Shell condones murder, all oil companies are single minded in their purpose. Maass recounts an interview with an anonymous French oil executive, who described the approach of oil companies as nothing short of empire-like.[97] Their sole goal is to make money.[98]

---

92. Maass, *Crude World*, 141.
93. Maass, *Crude World*, 141.
94. Chomsky, *Hegemony or Survival*, 130.
95. Maass, *Crude World*, 54–55.
96. Maass, *Crude World*, 71.
97. Maass, *Crude World*, 107.
98. Maass, *Crude World*, 131.

The enforcing of trade ensures a flow of resources back to the centre of empire. Early British involvement in Iran saw more taxes returning to the UK than going to Tehran. Likewise, when Iraq was invaded, Halliburton received large contracts for its reconstruction, not Iraqi firms. Halliburton was the former employer of the then U.S. Vice President, Dick Cheney.[99] A similar dynamic has been observed in Equatorial Guinea. There, oil companies provide little employment for locals, with crews and supplies to build facilities and feed staff, all imported.[100] Oil companies also take advantage of government naivety and pay small fees for oil concessions where possible, instead bribing officials and effectively supporting dictators and internal social inequality, giving rise to further conflict.[101] More money leaves oil countries, together with the oil, than enters the local economy.

Australia has not directly engaged in violence to secure access to East Timorese resources. However, it has effectively treated Indonesia as a pliant vassal, although mistakenly so, and was willing to turn a blind eye to government led violence and persecution. For its own part, in attempting to restrict the flow of information outside of East Timor, or re-spin it, Australia has been complicit in Indonesia's actions. In its constant fraudulent negotiations over maritime boundaries, the Australian government has explicitly acted in an imperial fashion, seeking to gain access to resources it had no right to. This included selling concessions to oil companies before boundaries were settled. In engaging in espionage, the Australian government were perpetrating a form of violence against another sovereign nation.

Oil geopolitics and the gospel

The Lordship of governments can be extractive, polluting, violent and corrupt. Oil does not bring the benefits it promises the nations where it is extracted, and oil is damaging our global climate. In contrast, the Lordship of Christ is serving, sacrificial and sustaining. Quite apart from deconstructing the violent methods of oil extraction, or draw-

---

99. Mark Gongloff, 'Iraq Rebuilding Contracts Awarded', *CNN Money* (25 March 2003), <http://money.cnn.com/2003/03/25/news/companies/war_contracts/>. Accessed 6 September 2015.
100. Maass, *Crude World*, 33-34.
101. Maass, *Crude World*, 36-52.

ing attention to the way in which creation has suffered, the gospel calls for another way of being entirely. This age of abundant oil is coming to an end, and so should the accompanying idea of infinite growth. As Pope Francis has noted:

> we do need to slow down and look at reality in a different way, to appropriate the positive and sustainable progress which has been made, but also to recover the values and the great goals swept away by our unrestrained delusions of grandeur (*LS* 114).[102]

This means addressing the myths of modernity which are grounded in a utilitarian mindset: individualism, unlimited progress, competition, consumerism, the unregulated market. Pope Francis also observes that 'the present ecological crisis is one small sign of the ethical, cultural and spiritual crisis of modernity' (*LS* 119).

To reimagine our entire way of life may seem an over whelming task, but a post-oil world will be very different from the world we have become accustomed to. Oil has fuelled enormous growth in western economies, but it has also wrought great environmental harm. Oil use will peak as resources decline, but oil use could also drop as warming precipitates a general collapse of civilisation. Far better that humanity should transition away from oil and fossil fuels in a more controlled manner. This will necessarily require rethinking and reimagining society.

This re-imagination will include rethinking geopolitics. The lordship of Caesar, with its violent or coercive acquisition of resources will need to give way to a more global cooperation. Given the historical debt of Western oil extraction and usage, Pope Francis is correct to note that 'developed countries ought to help pay this debt by significantly limiting their consumption of non-renewable energy and by assisting poorer countries to support policies and programmes of sustainable development'. (*LS* 52). Bird notes that righteousness is at the centre of Paul's proclamation of the gospel in Rom 1:16–17. Latin speaking hearers may have also heard echoes of *iustitita* (justice) and *aequitas* (fairness). Central to the gospel is the impartial vindication

---

102. *Encyclical Letter Laudato Si' of The Holy Father Francis on Care for Our Common Home*, Vatican Press, 24 May 2015 (abbreviated as *LS*).

of both Jew and Gentile.[103] The Lordship of Christ is one of justice. This essay has outlined the injustices perpetrated by Western powers in their unjust and often times violent acquisition of the oil resources of the developing nations. It is evident that both the benefits of fossil fuel use have not been fairly distributed and the resulting impacts of climate change are felt most by those least responsible. It is therefore a matter of Christian duty to repay the historical debts incurred by fossil fuel extraction and use.

The Pax Christi is nothing like the Pax Romana or Pax Americana, and a sharing of energy technologies will help replace the violent acquisition of energy resources that now takes place. Indeed, solar technology reminds us that 'He causes His sun to rise on the evil and the good' (Mt 5:45, NASB). Abandoning oil as a resource will necessarily mean a shift in power away from some currently oil rich or heavily oil dependent countries, as well as a number of influential multinational companies. It will also mean the abandonment of the associated military force as a foreign policy tool. Abandoning the mythos of endless growth will make moving away from oil easier. As Ivan Illich has put it, we need to reassert shalom against the domination of peace by *pax economica*, with its assumptions of scarcity, endless development, violence against nature, and so on.[104] The Church should be at the forefront of declaring that the Caesar that is the fossil fuel industry has no clothes. Fossil fuels have promised economic growth, but without consideration of the environmental impacts. The fossil fuel industry has long been aware of climate change, but has actively sought to cast doubt on the science.[105] The wedding of church and state in a Constantinian union has too often produced a union of civil religion that has promoted rather than questioned war, for example, as was demonstrated by U.S. willingness to support Saudi Arabia or to invade Iraq. Abandoning oil will provide one less reason for armed conflict. With the band Live, we can affirm that nothing is 'more godless than a war … so what are we fighting for?'[106]

---

103. Bird, 'One Who Will Arise to Rule over the Nations', 156.
104. Ivan Illich, *In the Mirror of the Past* (London: Marion Boyars Publishers, 1992).
105. McKenzie Funk, 'Did Exxon Lie about Global Warming', *Rolling Stone* (30 June 2016), <http://www.rollingstone.com/politics/news/did-exxon-lie-about-global-warming-20160630>. Accessed 12 October 2016.
106. Dahlheimer, Gracey, Kowalczyk, and Taylor, 'What Are We Fighting For?

Contributors

Joseph Camilleri is Emeritus Professor at La Trobe University, where he held the Chair in International Relations and was founding Director of the Centre for Dialogue, La Trobe University (2006–2012). He has written some 20 major books and more than 100 book chapters and journal articles. Recent publications include: *The UN Alliance of Civilizations in Asia-South Pacific: Current Context and Future Pathways* (2014); *Human Security Matters* (2012); *Culture, Religion and Conflict in Muslim Southeast Asia* (Routledge 2013); and *Religion and Ethics in a Globalizing World: Conflict, Dialogue and Transformation* (Palgrave MacMillan, 2011). Professor Camilleri is a Fellow of the Australian Academy of Social Sciences and Executive Director of Alexandria Agenda, a new venture in ethical consulting.

Keith Dyer teaches New Testament at Whitley College, and is an Associate Professor of the University of Divinity. He is the author of *The Prophecy on the Mount (Mk 13)* (1998) and co-editor of *Resurrection and Responsibility* (2009). He was Chair of the Academic Board of the University of Divinity (2005–2009), Secretary of the Fellowship for Biblical Studies (2013–2015), and a participant in the Colloquium on Material Culture and Religion in Macedonia (2013) and Turkey (2014). He is New Testament Editor for the *Australian Biblical Review*.

Anne Elvey is an honorary research associate of Trinity College Theological School, University of Divinity, and an adjunct research fellow in the School of Languages, Literatures, Cultures and Linguistics, Monash University. She is author of *The Matter of the Text:*

Material Engagements between Luke and the Five Senses (2011) and *An Ecological Feminist Reading of the Gospel of Luke: A Gestational Paradigm* (2005), and co-editor of *Climate Change—Cultural Change: Religious Responses and Responsibilities* (2013) and *Reinterpreting the Eucharist: Explorations in Feminist Theology and Ethics* (2013). Her research interests are in ecological hermeneutics, ecological poetics and biblical literature. She is managing editor of *Plumwood Mountain: An Australian Journal of Ecopoetry and Ecopoetics.*

Deborah Guess is an ecotheologian, a research associate and lecturer in Christianity and Ecology with Pilgrim Theological College, University of Divinity. Her publications include: "Deep Incarnation: A Resource for Ecological Christology", in *Climate Change, Cultural Change: Religious Responses and Responsibilities*, edited by Anne Elvey and David Gormley-O'Brien (Mosaic Books, 2013).

Shelini Harris is a scholar in the field of peace and conflict studies and religious studies addressing the way we relate to the environment as an integral part of peace structures. This includes studying the relationship between spirituality, values and sustainable lifestyles. Publications include: "Moral and Spiritual Change as a Basis for a Shift to Ecological Integrity: The Amish and Buddhists," in *Climate Change, Culture Change: Religious Responses and Responsibilities*, edited by Anne Elvey and David Gormley-O'Brien (Mosaic Books, 2013), and contributor to the report on 'Auroville Township and Ecovillage', in *Sustainable [R]evolution: Permaculture in Ecovillages, Urban Farms, and Communities Worldwide*, edited by Juliana Birnbaum and Louis Fox (North Atlantic Books, 2014).

John C McDowell is based in Melbourne as the Director of Research at the University of Divinity. He is an Executive Committee member of the University of Divinity's Centre for Research in Religion and Social Policy, a teaching accredited member of both Catholic Theological College and Yarra Theological Union, Associate Editor and Books Review Editor of the ANZATS journal *Colloquium*, and Executive Committee member of the journal *Pacifica: Journal of Theological Studies*. Among other things, he has authored *Hope in Barth's Eschatology: Interrogations and Transformations Beyond Tragedy* (Ashgate, 2000); *The Gospel According to Star Wars: Faith, Hope* *and the Force* (Westminster John Knox Press, 2007); *The Politics of Big Fantasy: Studies in Cultural Suspicion* (McFarland Press, 2014); and *The Ideology of Identity Politics in George Lucas* (Jefferson, NC: McFarland Press, 2016). He has edited *Philosophy and the Burden of Theological Honesty: A Donald MacKinnon Reader* (Continuum T&T Clark, 2011); and has co-edited *Kenotic Ecclesiology: Select Writings of Donald M. MacKinnon* with Ashley John Moyse and Scott A. Kirkland (Fortress Press, 2016); *Correlating Sobernost: Conversations Between Karl Barth and the Russian Orthodox Tradition* with Ashley John Moyse and Scott A. Kirkland (Fortress Press, 2016); and *Conversing with Barth* with Mike Higton (Ashgate, 2004). Among his main ethical concerns have been issues of human formation in and through nationalism, economic globalisation, and popular cultural artefacts; critical pedagogy and the corporatisation of higher education; and the ontologies of violent ideologies.

Mick Pope has degrees in mathematics, physics, meteorology and theology. He is a lecturer in meteorology, and eco-theologian with Ethos: EA Centre for Christianity and Society. Mick has several book chapters and published papers in ecotheology, and co-authored (with Claire Dawson), *A Climate of Hope: Church and Mission in a Warming World*.

Dianne Rayson is a Flechtheim Scholar completing her PhD at the University of Newcastle, Australia, on Bonhoeffer's contribution to ecotheology and ecoethics. She is on the board of the International Bonhoeffer Society, English Language Section, and has degrees in public health and theology. Dianne has published several papers and her most recent chapter (with Terence Lovat) is 'Bonhoeffer's Ecotheological Ethic and the Gandhi Factor', in *The Nature of Things: Rediscovering the Spiritual in God's Creation*, edited by Graham Buxton and Norman Habel (Wipf & Stock, 2016).

Asmi Wood is an Associate Professor at the Australian National University. He is a member of the ARC funded National Indigenous Research and Knowledges Network (NIRAKN).

Printed by Libri Plureos GmbH in Hamburg,
Germany